"Any parent or caregiver supporting a chil
knows their own needs are often overl
achieved in this inspirational yet practical guide is to offer concrete tools for parents and professionals alike. *From Exhausted to
Energized* not only shares the latest in Applied Behavioral Analysis
but offers the innovative and cutting-edge tools of mindfulness and
Emotional Freedom Techniques for self-care. This book will truly
enhance the life of any medical professional or family member caring for someone and is a must-read."

—Peta Stapleton, PhD
Clinical and Health Psychologist, Chair of Graduate
Research, Bond University, and author of *The Science
Behind Tapping: A Proven Stress Management Technique
for the Mind and Body*

"Since Leo Kanner's seminal 1943 paper on *infantile autism,* the
field of helping autistic people has advanced way beyond those
humble beginnings of the advent of Applied Behavioral Analysis
that is now integrated with Energy Psychology and mindfulness
methods. Mandi Freger's *From Exhausted to Energized: A Guide
for Caregivers of Children and Adults with Autism Spectrum Disorder* is an amazing reference guide for autism professionals and
caregivers, perhaps most of all for her reflection on the advance-
ments in compassionate treatment and self-care. Mandi does a
wonderful job with this labor of love. I highly recommend it."

—Fred P. Gallo, PhD, DCEP
Author of *Energy Psychology* and *The Tapping Toolbox*

"Effectively caring for people with Autism Spectrum Disorder without burning out requires an almost alchemical combination of
non-ordinary ways of supporting those with ASD and consistent
dedication to using powerful self-care methods for one's self. *From
Exhausted to Energized: A Guide for Caregivers of Children and*

Adults with Autism Spectrum Disorder shows you how to do both. You'll discover potent ways to effectively support people on the Spectrum while opening up to their autism—that becomes your own gift of growth. This is the book I wish my parents had when I was growing up."

—**David Gruder, PhD, DCEP**
Best-selling author, CEO of Integrity Culture Systems™, Director of The Center for Enlightened Self-Sovereignty, and Founding President of the Association for Comprehensive Energy Psychology

"Truly Inspirational! *From Exhausted to Energized* is a must-read for any caregiver or parent with a child with ASD. As a parent with a child on the autism spectrum, I know too well how we often lose ourselves, grow weary, and experience a level of PTSD. Mandi has written a fantastic book, providing specific tools to help us reduce our stress and regain our life."

—**Jennifer Giustra-Kozek, M.ED., LPC, CIMHP**
Author of *Healing Without Hurting: Treating ADHD, Apraxia, and Autism Spectrum Disorders Naturally and Effectively Without Harmful Medications.*

"As an owner of mental health clinics specializing in ASD and family therapy for 30 years, I guarantee this one-of a kind book is long overdue. Parents and guardians can learn a masterful weave of EP techniques and traditional methods! While it is written for ASD families, I believe all my families will benefit from Ms. Freger's insights. I'll be stocking my shelves with this book for clinician self-care and recommending it to all families for support."

—**Carole Stern, MS, RN-BC, DCEP**
Psychologist, Past President of ACEP, Certified Trauma Therapist, EFT Trainer

"In this seminal work, Ms. Freger reveals knowledge of how to take care of your ASD child and yourself, the parent/caregiver, that she acquired over decades of professional experience. For the first time, she reveals how to successfully combine standard psychological treatments, such as Applied Behavior Analysis and Discrete Trial Learning, with vibrant and effective trauma-based energy psychology interventions. These are known to have amazing benefits for both the ASD sufferer and caregivers.

Drawing from her extensive experience in treating and training professionals, parents, and children, Ms. Freger gives both clinical and research-guided step-by-step instructions for effectively remediating the overwhelming stress, trauma, and burnout so often experienced by parents and caregivers of ASD affected persons. She introduces the reader to the world of human energy fields, gives detailed instruction in identifying the 7 Caregiver Types, and supplies new effective tools necessary for revitalizing both our physical and emotional energy. This book is a must-read for anyone seeking to be an effective helper to those experiencing the social and communication challenges of those on the Autism Spectrum."

—Gregory J. Nicosia, PhD
Author of *Comprehensive Introduction to Thought Field Therapy*

FROM
EXHAUSTED
TO
ENERGIZED

FROM EXHAUSTED TO ENERGIZED

A Guide for Caregivers of Children and Adults with Autism Spectrum Disorder

Amanda Freger, M.ED., DCEP, LBS, LPC

SelectBooks, Inc.
New York

This edition published by SelectBooks, Inc.
For information address SelectBooks, Inc., New York, New York.

First Edition

ISBN 978-1-59079-567-5

Library of Congress Cataloging-in-Publication Data

Names: Freger, Amanda, author.
Title: From exhausted to energized : a guide for caregivers of children and adults with autism spectrum disorder / Amanda Freger, M.Ed., DCEP, LBS, LPC.
Description: First edition. | New York : SelectBooks, [2024] | Includes bibliographical references and index. | Summary: "Mandi Freger's 25 years of experience in the field of Energy Psychology enabled her to become skilled in the art of using energy therapeutic techniques with her patients; practices that enhanced her leadership roles in behavioral health treatment, specifically for those who are caretakers of patients with Autism Spectrum Disorder (ASD), trauma, and other cognitive dysfunctions"-- Provided by publisher.
Identifiers: LCCN 2024027187 (print) | LCCN 2024027188 (ebook) | ISBN 9781590795675 (paperback) | ISBN 9781590795682 (ebook)
Subjects: LCSH: Autism spectrum disorders in children--Treatment--Popular works. | Energy psychology--Popular works. | Autism spectrum disorders--Treatment--Popular works. | Children with autism spectrum disorders--Care--Popular works. | Autistic people--Care--Popular works.
Classification: LCC RJ506.A9 F6923 2024 (print) | LCC RJ506.A9 (ebook) | DDC 618.92/85882--dc23/eng/20240628
LC record available at https://lccn.loc.gov/2024027187
LC ebook record available at https://lccn.loc.gov/2024027188

Book design by Janice Benight

Manufactured in the United States of America
10 9 8 7 6 5 4 3 2 1

Contents

Introduction

Caring for Those with the Unique Characteristics of Autism Spectrum Disorder

Do you feel like you are lacking the skills you need to handle the massive task of caring for a person who's been diagnosed with autism spectrum disorder (ASD)? Is your motivation dwindling? Do you feel more and more that you are too drained to handle the never-ending quantity of tasks you've taken on? Or do you simply feel thoroughly exhausted and drained and have a hard time facing the day, feeling you are not equipped to tackle your To-Do list with any success.

Almost every caregiver of someone with ASD—whether or not they're a parent—inevitably runs into the proverbial brick wall as they try to juggle an alternative reality of out-of-control behaviors, communication difficulties, the child's unwavering demands and emotional upsets. Add to this the unexpected social reactions of others restrictive school settings, and it's not surprising we feel our society doesn't even come close to preparing us to have the wisdom, skills, and support to fulfill our herculean responsibilities as a caregiver. Much less do we feel we've been empowered with insights and practices that help us feel there's still something in our gas tank at the end of the day.

So how, in our technologically advanced and "enlightened" age, can caregivers stop feeling like they're running on fumes and start to feel like they are handling their demands and responsibilities—and succeeding to do well at them—and have found ways to have time for themselves?

That's exactly what this book will tell you.

Here's the thing. Caring for the population of people with autism spectrum disorder is unique; it's different from giving care to any other population. Although there are some overlaps with others, both psychologically and behaviorally, this group has unique characteristics that are especially intense and demanding of a caregiver. ASD affects virtually every aspect of the child's life—and continues into their adult life, remaining for their lifetime. And as the child grows and matures, the caregiver's responsibilities don't lessen—they just change. There's no getting around the fact that being a caregiver of someone with ASD will likely ask more of you than you thought you had to give.

How do we define a caregiver? In the following pages, I use the term to include anyone who works with, interacts with, or provides care to a person with ASD. This includes parents and other relatives, guardians, teachers, and a variety of types of therapists and other helpers. But for the most part, I am talking to parents since their job is 24/7/365 days a year with a twofold purpose of providing good parenting and managing the symptoms of the diagnosis. Being a parent caregiver is the most grueling, daunting, and demanding role of all.

To the general public, it sure seems like the incidence of autism spectrum disorder is increasing in the United States. In 2021, the Centers for Disease Control and Prevention reported that approximately one in 44 children in the U.S. is diagnosed with an ASD, based on 2018 data, although the sample was limited. Data from a 2014 study reported one in 59 children, and a study from 2010, reported one child in 68 children at that time. And the further back we go in time, the more reduced the numbers are.

People frequently ask me why I think the prevalence of ASD is increasing and, in fact, doing so at a staggering rate. Why is this ? I believe that the numbers reflect the fact that there's an increased awareness of the diagnostic criteria and assessments of the unique aptitudes, emotional sensitivities, and behaviors that are the symptoms of ASD— yet I also believe that it has been around for a long time. People just didn't know what to call it or how to manage it in their families and schools. Psychologists and medical doctors also didn't know how to treat people with it. Up until the 1980s—when the American Psychiatric Association began to define autism as a separate diagnosis of a mental disorder—people with ASD symptoms were simplistically seen as being "weird" or "cold," too "business-like" or "super-structured." Or they were diagnosed with a laundry list of other mental health diagnoses that didn't fully or accurately apply to them and were nonetheless placed in a specific category of pathology.

It wasn't until the 1990s, that practitioners began to diagnose people with autism, and later, with the name autism spectrum disorder. Many years ago, when I worked in Pittsburgh, the University of Pittsburgh Medical Center, which was a regional hub for genetics research and diagnosis at the time, was one of only a few facilities in my region where psychologists or diagnosticians were using comprehensive assessments and willing to give this diagnosis. Many kids were taken to that facility to get a diagnosis. These days, I see more and more diagnoses coming from independent psychologists, psychiatrists, and clinicians with better screening tools available and being used in pediatrics. As the industry has provided more precise definitions, more clinicians are well informed and trained to give this diagnosis.

Think about it. For most of the last two centuries, our culture has been founded on rules that were pretty black-and-white. At the same time, the ASD population happens to perform well in a black-and-white rules-oriented environment. So a lot of people—beginning in childhood and then well beyond—dropped under the radar and were not noticed. When you were growing up, did you notice kids in school that just seemed quirky? Or maybe you never saw them again because they ended up in a separate program in your school. Those profoundly affected with the disorder might have been residents at psychiatric institutions, helping to explain why those institutions were so full at that time. In some areas, adult children continued to live at home, getting their care from family members, and considered to have "special needs" because of the lack of understanding of the nuances of the disorder back then. Many were simply labeled mentally retarded and were sharply segregated into special education.

Still, as the numbers of diagnoses climb, there are often not enough resources to meet the needs of this population and help their families to understand the disorder and succeed in managing it. The layers of a child's problematic behaviors that are visible are often combined with their unseen internal difficulties of struggling with cognitive and emotional problems. When this is overlooked, it's very easy to mistake their symptoms for other diagnoses. That's why I consider it so crucial to not only teach more outpatient clinicians how to work with this population but to provide caregivers with a set of tools that will educate them and hone their skills to do the best for the child as well as themselves.

Autism spectrum disorder is incredibly complex, layered with many features, and it varies significantly from one person to the next. It knows no boundaries; no culture or ethnic group has been identified as having higher rates of ASD. As Dr. Stephen Shore said: "If you've met one person with autism, you've met one person with autism." It can be very misleading to try to generalize and think that you know anything about someone just because you know the name of their diagnosis. As a result, the general public remains largely in the dark about most facets of their state of being and makes erroneous assumptions based on only a superficial brush with it in their lives or through consumption of what the media broadcasts.

It's also important to point out three things: all of us fall somewhere on a larger continuum of mental health and functionality, there's an extraordinary degree of diversity within the human species, and each one of us is unique. Just as no sub-group of humans are all alike, those with ASD are not all alike. It's one reason why I sometimes like to refer to those who have not been diagnosed with ASD as "non-spectrum spectrumers" rather than "neurotypical."

Thankfully, treatment of autism spectrum disorder has come a long way in the past few decades. This book will give you insights into some of the skills that professionals use to work with people who are diagnosed with ASD. You'll gain insight into the scientific understanding of what is going on in the brains of those diagnosed with ASD and learn what behaviorists and clinicians understand about behavior—how both "good" and "bad" behavior—is activated. You'll learn what professionals look for in the behaviors of people on the autism spectrum so they can begin to determine why certain behaviors arise in the first place. These insights will inspire and empower you to be much more effective as a caretaker when you are confronted by the often mysterious and frustrating behaviors of the child you are caring for.

I hope you will also spend time looking honestly at the many layers of stress and anxiety that inevitably come with the package of providing care to a person with ASD. If you're going to stop your energy from hemorrhaging and feel alive again, you need to understand what you're dealing with. I'll review the multi-faceted challenges you face as a caregiver so you can understand that you're not alone and can also appreciate the depth of the task before you.

I've included loads of recommendations about how to be more effective as a caregiver—both at home, when you're parenting or supervising and when you're working with a behavioral team at school. The insights I provide will help you become a more informed and active participant as you engage in developing your child's treatment plans and forwarding their behavioral and educational goals. And you'll be in a much better place to monitor their progress, so you'll feel more confident and in control of the process.

Finally, I'll teach you how to recognize the three components of effectiveness for the caregivers. These are the areas that you can directly control and manage, and as a result, they'll help you recharge your batteries, manage your reserves, and understand how to optimize your health as you give so generously to others. I'll help you understand the chief skills you need to do that and explain how your willingness can impede or facilitate your efforts. I'll give you simple exercises that will allow you to keep your energy reserves strong and resilient. With the help of mindfulness and energy work, you can maximize your skills, build your confidence, and become more effective. And you'll have more time for yourself at the end of the day.

Being a caregiver of a person with ASD challenges you to unfold layers of yourself, and as you are faced with your weaknesses and forced to embrace change, you are given the opportunity to strengthen and empower yourself in new, meaningful ways that will last a lifetime. Yes, you can be an excellent, responsive, and effective caregiver and still feel more alive and energized than you ever imagined you could be.

Let me show you how.

1

A Journey into
the World of Treatments

remember my introduction to autism. When I was a teenager, my mother and my aunt were elementary school teachers in the public school system in southwestern Pennsylvania. One day they were tossing around their ideas about how to troubleshoot learning problems they observed in their classes, and my aunt mentioned one of her students was "autistic." I was an assertive and nerdy adolescent, so I tried to correct her.

"Did you mean *artistic*?" I asked.

"No," my aunt said. "I meant *autistic*," emphasizing the first syllable more than necessary for me to hear the difference. Their conversation continued about a child with a novel diagnosis and how the staff was scrambling to devise some kind of support program for him. Little did I know how complicated a diagnosis of autism was or much less how profoundly familiar I'd become with it.

For as long as I can remember, all I ever wanted to do "when I grew up" was to somehow be a person of service in the field of medicine. I envisioned a single-track career path in front of me, a straight line to my desired goal, so I didn't need to come up with a backup plan. When it was time for me to go to college, I dove into biology, chemistry, and math—all in alignment with my intention to go into pre-med right after graduation.

But then life got in the way of my plans. When I was a junior in college, my father fell ill, and I was faced with a series of difficult choices regarding my career path and my close relationship with him.

It seemed the best thing to do was to move back to my hometown and transfer my studies to St. Vincent College in Latrobe, Pennsylvania, which was close to home. As I watched my dad's health decline precipitously, I realized I wanted to whatever I could to make it possible for him to see me graduate from college—and I needed to accomplish this before it was too late. I had to somehow finish my studies quickly. With a heavy heart and a determination not to look back, I decided to switch my major to Liberal Arts; the change meant I would be able to graduate just one semester later than I would have in my current undergraduate program. But my future—something that had once been clearly defined—was now a complete mystery to me.

Once out of school, I needed a job, one that was not likely to be in the field of medicine—some employment I had never expected to seek or was prepared to look for. But in a streak of good fortune, my cousin told me of an opening in the facility where she was working. TBI Neuro-Rehabilitation, a facility treating adults with mild to profound traumatic brain injuries, was seeking someone to fill the position of Resident Advisor, known as an RA. It seemed intriguing to me, so I interviewed for and got the job.

The company offered treatment services day and night. Their day program provided TBI patients with vocational and/or cognitive rehab. Then, at night, Resident Advisors like me would take the residents back to the apartments that the company had set up for their patients and spend time with them to help retrain them in some basic life skills.

To prepare me for the job, the company put me through several hours of orientation training and had me shadow more experienced RAs so I could learn general crisis management skills to deal with aggressive or unsafe behaviors. Those few hours hardly prepared me for the eruptions that would often take place, but I somehow still remained open to learning by experience.

I was working with only one or two residents each night, so I was afforded the time and space to observe their behaviors. Sure, I was there to help keep them safe, but I was also in a position to watch for patterns and other factors setting off their behaviors. Sometimes I even got a sense of what they were seeing through their eyes. I noticed that escalations arose most often at times of confusion or cognitive misunderstandings. Or incidents would occur when the resident was over-focused and couldn't set something aside. Being in that observer position helped me recognize the complexity involved in cognitive issues and helped me see that, as much as there were behaviors they had in common, each person's symptoms, patterns, and behaviors were quite different and unique.

I was 22 years old, the youngest RA working there at the time, and the volatility of the residents I worked with was sometimes overwhelming. To deal with this tension, I got firm with myself. "No one else is afraid or has a problem with this job," I told myself. "So you better just get over it." I quickly taught myself to think of this population's unpredictable and aggressive behavior as their "normal." After all, these were adults with severe brain injuries, so impulsiveness came with the package. Little did I know that this piece of wisdom would become a very valuable tool in crisis management and would serve me well for years to come.

Even with the challenges of the job, there was something about it I felt an affinity for. The organization was in the midst of expanding, too, and I wanted to be a part of it—perhaps even move up within the company. To that end, based on the advice of a psychologist on staff, I entered a master's degree program in educational psychology at Indiana University of Pennsylvania. It didn't require an internship, so it wouldn't be too demanding of my time. However, I took the extra time I did have to circle back to my undergraduate program and complete the work that was needed so I could obtain a certification in business management in addition to my master's. As it turned out, that would be helpful later on, too.

Interestingly enough, the psychologist on staff inadvertently opened up more doors for me at the company. She left her job shortly after we spoke in order to take a higher position with a company that was closer to her home. Then, about a year later, she contacted me to find out how I was doing and to see if I was about finished earning my master's degree.

"Yes," I told her.

"Well, we need someone to do assessments and cognitive testing at the practice in Pittsburgh—basically, someone to do what I do now—but working under me. What do you think about interviewing for the job?" It sounded great to me.

The practice was called Advanced Diagnostics, P.C., and the owner was psychologist Dr. Gregory Nicosia, who, I soon discovered, is one of the world's true visionaries in the field of energy psychology. Energy psychology, or EP, is a collection of methods that use the body's electromagnetic system to leverage the mind-body connection and accelerate healing results. Dr. Nicosia had developed a technique called Thought Energy Synchronization Therapy (TEST™), an offshoot of Thought Field Therapy®, which is designed to reduce psychological upsets by removing energetic blocks that impede the smooth flow of energy in the body.

I came to realize that so much more had been happening under the TBI umbrella than I knew, even though I had been working for the company for a year. Dr. Nicosia had a multidisciplinary team offering neuropsychological assessments, cognitive rehabilitative therapies, QEEG testing, chiropractic, and other services. He was also a board-certified forensic examiner and submitted reports and depositions for courts to use in traumatic brain injury-related litigation. In my new position in the company, I was to assist in completing neuropsychological testing that he'd need for those reports.

Nicosia offered several levels of courses in his TEST curriculum, and the most advanced course involved diagnostic techniques. He trained me in all levels of TEST and I soon found it quite practical and effective. It was my first exposure to a fairly concrete tool—under the umbrella of what we now collectively call "energy psychology"—that could be used to help reduce unpleasant feelings clients had about their issues and thus broaden their perspective about their problematic situation. After a client received energy psychology sessions, changes in thoughts and behavior would often follow.

My newly acquired mastery of TEST protocols had opened a new world to me. My master's program had mostly focused on theoretical perspectives and strategies for navigating cognitive issues and facilitating behavior modification. I was loving the more hands-on direction in which I was heading. Dr. Nicosia also recommended that I get training in Eye Movement Desensitization and Reprocessing (EMDR), another psychotherapeutic method that helps people recover from trauma. In short order, I completed formal training in Level I and Level II EMDR.

◆ ◆ ◆ ◆ ◆

Now working as a psychotherapist at Advanced Diagnostics, P.C., I began to build a small caseload of clients whose diagnoses ranged from cognitive disorders and PTSD to depression, anxiety, and chronic pain. The new techniques I'd learned proved to be quite effective, and my work was making an impact. I was now able to implement traditional cognitive rehabilitation strategies that I saw the psychologist use at my old job to help retrain memory, along with other cognitive strategies. Now, I could add in energy psychology tools if the tasks became too overwhelming. At the time, Dr. Nicosia was just starting to travel around the country, training people in his TEST methods, and he asked me to help him with the scheduling, marketing, and outreach for those programs in addition to the work I was doing with clients.

As his seminars continued to get more popular in the industry and attendance grew, he asked me to help lead some small groups of practice sessions within the seminars, too. I was getting very good at his therapeutic methods, but in spite of this recognition of my skills, I would sometimes get pushback from the attendees. There I was, at 24, helping mature and diversely trained doctoral-level psychologists learn a new psychological technique—and some of them doubted my expertise. A handful of people even asked me my age, sure that it wasn't possible for me to know about something in their field of expertise when I had so little experience in it. (My response was to suggest that we just get through what we needed to learn, and if they still cared how old I was when we were done, I'd tell them then. But they usually had forgotten about it by that point!)

I looked around and realized I had been fortunate to find myself in a job where I could spend endless hours getting coached and mentored by one of the most respected leaders in energy-based psychotherapeutic treatments of trauma and cognitive dysfunctions.

Between rides in cars and airplanes and the hours of downtime we had between trainings, I also had the luxury of being able to listen to Dr. Nicosia describe the power and energy of our thoughts. He shared with me the principles behind Thought Field Therapy® that make it so effective, the human patterns that we can predict and manage, and the decision tree we can use to navigate what steps to take to dismantle them if we want to.

I ate it up. It just all made sense. He was pointing in the direction of a whole new untapped field that, little did I know, was just about to emerge in the world.

It was also interesting to me that people coming to his facility were coming from a medical community that was still steeped in the disease model. It was a shift for them to experience our integrative and holistic approach, to look at their own wellness, and to get better without just being prescribed a pill or physical therapy. Even though Pittsburgh was known for its cutting-edge hospitals, Nicosia was generally considered to have more in-depth skills than others to rapidly relieve complex issues to identify the underlying causes of emotional trauma linked to the patient's physical disease. Using his tools, it was possible to provide emotional releases that greatly impacted an individual's ease of recovery and ability to manage pain. His methods of treating emotional distress were much more advanced than those of the traditional medical and psychotherapeutic community at the time.

I came to appreciate that even more when I later spent some time working in facilities in surrounding counties and found out how well-known he was for his work. Years later, I would learn that his reputation went far beyond the state of Pennsylvania.

Then, somewhat suddenly, the licensure laws changed, and I could no longer continue to practice without a license, while solely under someone's supervision. In effect, I was forced out of my job, even though I had completed two years of great work at Advanced Diagnostics. I simply had to pack up and go.

Regardless of my master's degree in educational psychology and my training and experience in treatment modalities, I found myself taking odd jobs just to get by. After about a year, I saw an ad for a job opening at a company offering Behavioral Health and Rehabilitative Services (BHRS).[1] They offered therapeutic interventions that are provided to children and adolescents up to age 21 who have behavioral, emotional, or developmental disorders. In my region of Pennsylvania, I was taught that BHRS was initially designed to serve those with pervasive developmental disorders (PDDs)—a term that many used interchangeably with "autism" at the time—but the state expanded its services to treat youth who had been diagnosed with any DSM[2] diagnosis.

Family Behavioral Resources (FBR), a company with a large base in Westmoreland County, Pennsylvania, was looking to fill a job that encompassed two roles: behavior specialist consultant (BSC) and mobile therapist (MT). The list of required skills for the job was right up my alley—and the position didn't require a license. Just what I was looking for. At the time I took the interview, the company was fairly new, offering BHRS services and outpatient clinics with a team of about 20 employees at one Westmoreland County office. It would later grow into one of the biggest mental health services organizations in the state.

In Pennsylvania at that time, aside from early, non-intensive intervention for children up to age five, BHRS was the only community-based service for children diagnosed under the umbrella of pervasive developmental disorders from infancy up to 21 years of age who could get

---

1 BHRS also used to be interchangeable with "wraparound" services in PA.

2 *The Diagnostic and Statistical Manual of Mental Disorders* (DSM) is published by the American Psychiatric Association and is used for classification of all mental health disorders. From 1994 to 2013, the fourth edition, or "DSM-IV" was in use. In the fifth edition, or "DSM-V, "many of the definitions of what were formerly called pervasive developmental disorders were reorganized and revised under the term autism spectrum disorders.

state-supported professional help to develop behavioral skills. Commercial health care plans would not cover it; the only insurance that would was Pennsylvania's Medical Assistance (Medicaid) program, which provided 100 percent coverage regardless of the parents' income. On the one hand, it was a godsend. But the path that so many families had to take to get those services was often painful and complex. If the family didn't already have Medical Assistance, they'd have to make an appointment with a psychologist and get an evaluation and mental health diagnosis for the child, as any child would. However, they'd then have to take that diagnostic evaluation to the Social Security office, which would qualify them for Medical Assistance. But that was just the beginning.

Technically, it was up to the psychologist to determine at what age the child could start services and what intensity of services would be received. For example, they might write orders for the child to receive help at age two or three, and they might prescribe that the services take place for so many hours a week and for so many months—just like a medical prescription. But then Medical Assistance would often balk at the orders, claiming they weren't medically necessary and refuse to cover them or reduce the prescription significantly. Essentially, the family was at their mercy, without enough help or hope. They'd try to argue: "Hey, my doctor said my child needs this," but the care representatives for Medical Assistance wouldn't budge. Parents could challenge the care managers in a grievance process. The care managers would send the prescription to their physicians, who were employed by Medical Assistance, to review them and give their final blessing or they would agree to a reduced prescription. The physicians would meet with the initial prescribing clinician or the behavioral specialist to dispute the change. Usually, the final blessing and outcome was one and the same—the Medical Assistance physician's recommendation.

It should be noted that, initially, there were three levels to the grievance process, and it could take months. There was also what was called a "fair hearing," where parents had to defend themselves and their child's clinical presentation to qualified physicians. Talk about "intimidating."

Parents endured an emotional roller coaster ride just trying to get help for their kids.

Even for those who were approved for getting coverage for BHRS services, the distress usually continued. Historically, every three or four months, an insurance meeting was required to re-evaluate the child's qualifications for coverage, and parents had to put on a bit of a show to win them over. They had to walk a fine line, on the one hand, demonstrating that the kid was making progress; on the other, making it clear how impaired they still were, how much their safety was at risk, and how much they still needed the services to be provided to their kid. The BSC's role was to provide data that would support the engagement of services along with the psychologist's prescription.

When I interviewed with Family Behavioral Resources for the BSC position, I was shocked to discover that the staff people interviewing me were practitioners just like me—not licensed psychologists. They were my age! They asked a few questions, and when they asked me about the modalities I use in my practice, I told them, "EMDR and TFT." Methods I would later recognize as forms of energy psychology.

"What are those?" they asked.

I was surprised that they weren't familiar with them. After all, I had witnessed how effective they could be. Were they really unaware of such effective methods? The answer was Yes.

Then they told me that the job I was interviewing for would involve working with youth with autism and other diagnoses under the umbrella of pervasive developmental disorders, which would include PDD, NOS, Asperger's disorder, autistic disorder, Rhett's disorder, and childhood disintegrative disorder.

"Okay. Well, I don't know much about those, although I have a background in treating trauma. And I have experience treating cognitive disorders, anxiety and depression, ADHD, and more. Can't I just work with people with other diagnoses besides autism?"

They told me no, I could not.

"Well, can you tell me what I need to do with these kids? How to approach them?" I asked, trying to get a sense of where I could even begin.

"Behavior modification" was their simple answer.

I still needed more explanation. "Like what?"

They mentioned something about behavior modification techniques such as reinforcement and something about a "token economy," which is a positive-reinforcement behavioral approach that I remembered from graduate school, although it sounded too simplistic. I was surprised that they were only willing to point to a fairly superficial, simplistic approach to something that I suspected was going to be quite complex. I realized I'd just have to jump in and learn as I went.

• • • • •

In fact, I had a lot to learn about the types of disorders they were treating. According to the DSM-IV, which was in use at that time, there were five diagnoses under the category of pervasive developmental disorders (PDD): autistic disorder, Asperger's disorder, Rhett's disorder, childhood disintegrative disorder, and pervasive developmental disorder-not otherwise specified (PDD-NOS).[3] These diagnoses were generally defined as being evidenced by deficits in communication and socialization, and by odd repetitive behaviors that were difficult to correct. What struck me was that while other disorders—say, insomnia or binging/purging, for example—can be identified by a very specific set of behaviors, the PDD category seemed to touch virtually every aspect of a person's life: communication, socialization, behaviors. These seem to encompass a whole universe of human expression—and just about everything that a person does.

It was daunting to think about, and I wondered how you can work with such a large scope. My mind was whirling with questions. *Then, how do you even know where to start with these kids?* I wondered. *Do you use rewards? How do you measure if it's working?* And on and on. I soon learned that the agency—in fact, all agencies involved in behavior

---

3 In 2013, the American Psychiatric Association published the DSM-V, which eliminated the category of pervasive developmental disorders and merged five distinct diagnoses from the DSM-IV into one umbrella diagnosis of autism spectrum disorder (ASD). A diagnosis would also specify the degree of support required for care.

modification methods of these disorders—taught that the place to start was with safety issues. First and foremost, we had to make sure nobody was going to run out into traffic or climb onto anything unsafe or risk injury to themselves or anyone else. Those were the places to start. *But, I thought, if they are having trouble communicating, how do you even teach them safety?* If you could just tell a kid to stop running out in the street, and that's all it took, you'd just do this. But it wasn't going to be as simple as that with this population.

I could see that the road ahead would be complicated and perplexing. I would have to be patient with my lack of knowledge. I was being thrown into a first-hand learning environment about these disorders where I would need to grow my understanding as quickly as I could—and with little formal support besides the insights I got from my peers.

At FBR, I was given volumes of state regulations and best practice guidelines to read. In lieu of experiencing active training, I was given a three-inch "training binder" that contained discussions about ethics, crisis management, policies and procedures, and a little bit of clinical training guidance. The time spent with the binder counted as the required 15 hours of training for the job.

As a behavior specialist consultant and mobile therapist, I was responsible for training my direct intervention staff specifically for each child's case; I was also responsible for creating BHRS treatment plans for the kids. These would include a customized curriculum for each child that would include behavioral goals to build academic success as well as success with life skills. For example, they'd include skills that kids typically learn in school, such as colors, numbers, object identification, sight words, and so forth. Unfortunately, one point that is often missed about these types of programs is that the work specifically targets improvements in compliance and attention—capabilities that the kids need to build to develop skills such as identifying colors and numbers. Actually, learning these academic skills was a by-product of our success at working on teaching them to pay attention and comply with the teacher's instructions. On top of that, the curricula were also designed to address communication, socialization, and behavior issues.

I remained with Family Behavioral Resources for five years, and over that time the list of goals for these kids grew exponentially. When I started, we set five to ten goals to accomplish for each kid. But a few years later, we were more likely to aim for achieving 30 goals for each child. One cause of the change was that managed care insurance companies kept asking us to show more of what we were doing—making us target every single behavior—eating with utensils, sitting at the table, handwashing, using the toilet, etc.—as a goal. We were also bringing to light how much these kids actually needed to learn. We were getting better at what we were doing and found that after we started working with a kid we had greater insight into what they needed. In other words, they might have begun to learn their ABCs, and they might even have gotten caught up enough in the standard curriculum taught at their age to attend school. But at the same time, behaviors would emerge pointing to the many things they still needed to learn to be in a school system.

I was grateful that my master's program had taught me something about how people think and learn. I couldn't imagine how counselors who didn't have the more specific educational psychology background that I had could go about figuring out the best ways to help these children learn.

I also learned a lot from my peers. I was lucky enough to have a therapeutic staff support (TSS) colleague that had been trained in some methods I was not yet familiar with. I watched her implement the treatment plan and took note of some of the precise skills she was using to help the child learn. For one, she used very concrete, simple language, and she worked with them in a very quiet environment. This was a method I grew to appreciate more and more. In the years to come, I'd learn that when we're trying to teach these kids how to communicate with us and their classmates, we have to be super deliberate about every word we say. We don't want to waste words or even use formal precise sentences because they don't yet have a way to understand the connection of good grammar to communication. From the outside, it can look and sound a little weird sometimes. But as I watched our theories in practice, I thought it was pure genius. The kids stayed pretty calm and were able to sit still, attend classes, and learn!

The work became fascinating to me, and in just six months, I was promoted to the position of clinical supervisor in the organization, which had grown to about 60 people by then. Two years later, I was also given the title of Director of Outpatient Services, overseeing clinicians in roles that are more equivalent to outpatient therapy, and I managed their clinical documentation, or their formal client notes for the records.

At the time, I still felt like we were in the early stages of learning what it meant to treat autism, and I even breathed a sigh of relief, thinking the new position might mean I would no longer need to provide as much direct treatment, especially because of the managed care stipulations. But, of course, I was actually given more responsibility in the position because it was up to me to make sure other people knew what they were doing. I quickly learned that to get staff to respect me, I had to be proficient at what I did, and I had to fully understand how much they knew. Over the years, I witnessed many changes in the mental health system and became more familiar with the area resources and other mental health services in my state. Sadly, I also became very aware of the lack of training requirements for those treating people with these developmental disorders.

◆ ◆ ◆ ◆ ◆

After working for about five years at Family Behavioral Resources, I grew uncomfortable with all the turnover I was witnessing around the company. People were getting burned out from dealing with managed care and from working with families who needed more than they could give. I wanted to pivot and re-visit my energy psychology roots more intensively to see if I could make more of a difference there. I took a newly created position as a second shift residential supervisor at Adelphoi Village, a residential treatment facility for youth and their families.

Adelphoi Village housed many at-risk kids with criminal back-grounds and provided assessment, treatment, and supervision. My job as RS was to manage the 30 staff members in the three houses that worked with kids with mental health diagnoses. About two-thirds of the youth had experienced problems that resulted in court proceed-ings where judges or arbiters had determined their rights and obliga-tions. The rest of the children were not involved in court proceedings and were struggling with serious mental health issues that nevertheless caused them problems in the community.

The paramount goal of my position was to reduce the frequency of the use of physical restraints on these young people. At that time, Adelphoi Village—just like other similar facilities around the coun-try—were by and large reacting only to extreme behaviors in crisis situations; they were not managing or mitigating conflicts, and physi-cal restraint had become the default solution when things got physically out of control. To that end, the company had been seeking someone experienced with treating trauma at a time when the term "trauma-in-formed care" was only just beginning to emerge to collectively address this lack of knowledge. It had been a common aspect of my career so far—yet it was only just getting recognized as a valuable methodology in the industry. I was to train staff about trauma, teach them to de-es-calate crisis situations better, and, as a result, reduce the frequency of use of physical restraints.

Restraints required authorization by a psychiatrist and another licensed mental health professional. Every incident was extremely well-documented and noted by state regulators, and the statistics were regularly monitored. By educating their staff about effective treatments and interventions, the heads of Adelphoi Village were hoping to turn their "physical restraint" numbers around. Which is what I did. As the staff learned the methods I taught and implemented them, the restraint numbers dropped significantly.

But once again, in this mental health treatment environment, I started noticing complexities that weren't being addressed head-on. I observed that some of these teenagers had laundry lists of mental health diagnoses, yet hardly any of them were diagnosed with anything under the umbrella of pervasive developmental disorders. I also saw kids that I felt were glaringly misdiagnosed, which altered the way we approached crisis interventions with them. So, while I couldn't re-diagnose a kid, I could suggest to staff that they try a different kind of intervention. And that was part of my success with helping to raise the staff's level of skills.

There also seemed to be a stunning mismatch between the level of expertise needed to do those staff jobs and the background of the people they hired, who were high school graduates or had a bachelor's degree, even though some had experience working with adjudicated youth. Staff members needed to be able to manage young people to prevent them from needing acute care hospitalization.. They needed to learn how to de-escalate situations as skillfully as possible. It seemed obvious, but skill levels were directly related to effectiveness on the job.

On the other hand, I also noted that what matters at least as much as training or education is the willingness to learn the skills. Learning how to not react if someone is physically aggressing on you can be incredibly hard. It takes a special person, a special disposition, and a lot of practice. Willingness goes a long way, and, along with skill, willingness would end up figuring into my growing understanding of what it takes to not burn out on the job.

I taught the staff to work with many diagnoses—anxiety, depression, mood disorders, PTSD, schizophrenia, schizoaffective disorders, conduct disorders, oppositional defiant disorders, ADHD, and more. Of course, it wasn't the staff's job to do therapy with the kids; most of their time was spent working in groups. Sometimes there were 3 or 4 staff members to 10 kids. Keep in mind that the "kids" were usually at least 13 years old, often fully grown, and the staff was made up mainly of recent college graduates. This virtual peer-to-peer relationship made crisis management and physical interventions even more challenging. Since trauma is accompanied by other conditions, such as dissociation, attachment issues, or even psychosis, it might take 4 or 5 staff members to restrain a youth who was "acting out." While hospitals might opt for mechanical or chemical restraints, our only option was almost always physical restraint that to an outsider might look something like hand-to-hand combat. It was traumatic for everyone involved.

To reduce their need to use restraints, I taught the staff how to use their words, phrases, body positioning, and the tone of their voices to help the young patients change certain antagonistic behaviors. By changing their own habits, the members of our staff learned to manage their emotions to prevent the need to use physical intervention.

Since the focus of the organization was generally to treat youth who were at-risk of criminal behavior, there was of course, a prevailing criminal-justice mindset. This relied on a behaviorist model that emphasized choice-making and recognizing consequences as a result of their choices. But for our mental-health group, it fell short. It was a straightforward behaviorist model that didn't take these young people's feelings into account or consider that they might have an underlying internal conflict and confusion. It was based on a black-and-white solution: If an incident escalated, they would just reach for the shackles in the secure units. In my units, however, putting children in shackles was not appropriate as a first go-to solution .

Trauma-informed care involved many strategies. Some of the necessary basics included teaching them to see the world from the child's eyes and convincing them that the purpose of a restraint was not to show the child who is boss but to protect a person from harming themselves or others. While it was a practical approach, being exposed to provocative behaviors from the same kids for hours on end can be difficult to get through. Self-awareness and accountability to change one's own responses through traditional cognitive behavioral practices can help, but it was difficult for many of the staff to address this. Through an energy psychology lens, this awareness would be considered mindfulness.

One of the mantras I used early in my career was: "Pay attention and don't assume (anything)." A few of the kids were actually interested in learning some of the energy psychology tools, and I was permitted to work with some of them.

Because some of the staff had difficulty learning the foundational skills and had a resistance to change, it wasn't easy for all of them to wrap their heads around what I was teaching the kids. Even my own staff—many of them were big, strong guys—showed a bit of anger and resistance to my ideas when I was getting started. They thought I was suggesting that they needed to soften their approach, but I wasn't. I was teaching them how to intervene with these kids who had complex mental health issues—and to do it effectively. As a result, they didn't have to call the secure unit staff for assistance, telling them to bring their restraints along as they'd done as a matter of course in the past. After all, when a kid escalated an expression of strong feelings would sometimes take five guys to de-escalate the situation, and sadly, by using force. With the training I was giving them, they were learning effective intervention skills, and they, themselves, were able to prevent escalation in the first place and were better able to de-escalate situations on their own without force. Calls for restraints were happening less and less frequently.

Some of the staff actually expressed interest in learning how to moderate their own escalating feelings in these situations, so I also taught a few of them some basics about energy psychology, just for their own use. That helped them build resilience and shored up their ability to stay centered even when things got chaotic. When I used some EP tools with some of the residents, they really took to learning to empower themselves.

One girl, age 15, landed in our facility because she would have occasional seizures. Not all seizures are the type where someone drops to the ground and convulses. When she experienced seizures, she would suddenly become quite combative. It was not my first experience with this type of presentation. During a session with her, I asked her how we could help her when that happens since traditional methods of de-escalation had not been effective. Tearful and sounding hopeless, she said, "I don't know, but I will try anything." I told her I'd show her a few steps of a technique called Thought Field Therapy, which calls for light tapping on the face and body to clear energy pathways in the body. She said it felt really good.

As proactive intervention, I asked for her consent to tap on her when her emotions were rapidly accelerating because she probably wouldn't have the presence of mind to do it herself, and she said Yes. One day, this happened in my presence. A seizure came on, and she almost struck a staff member. As soon as I started the tapping technique, she literally stopped in her tracks. The other employees at Adelphoi Village couldn't believe what they saw. One second, she was ready to throw a punch, and the next, she was calm.

Soon after this, my supervisor came to see me because she was excited to show me a flyer she'd received about an upcoming seminar on energy psychology. And who was leading it? Dr. Gregory Nicosia. I went to the training, of course, and reconnected with him. As we talked, he mentioned that there were therapists doing energy psychology in my area that needed some professional support in their clinics. I was intrigued.

◆ ◆ ◆ ◆ ◆

About a year later, I got a call from someone Dr. Nicosia had referred to me. Carol Stern, a former psychiatric nurse and clinical psychologist who is the owner and CEO of The Stern Center for Behavioral and Developmental Health in Pittsburgh (referred to as TSC), wanted to hire me as Clinical Director at one of her satellite offices.

About that time, Pennsylvania started requiring behavior consultants to be licensed as behavioral specialists, apparently to improve the quality of care for people who were diagnosed under the category of Pervasive Developmental Disorders. I was grandfathered in and was among the first wave of practitioners that applied for it. But while the intentions might have been good, the requirement created some disheartening problems. First of all, it disrupted the services that families had been getting from unlicensed BSCs, even though the transition was implemented gradually. And the BSC licensing requirement also created a difficult dilemma for the licensed professionals trained and skilled to take care of the spectrum population after the initial grandfathering period. The criteria to become licensed were nearly as stringent as those that professional counselors and social workers had to fulfill to be able to practice independently under their own licenses. Most of the people who qualified for the BSC license after the grandfathering period already held a license in another clinical discipline.

This meant they could decide to work as a BSC in a BHRS position for about $20 to $30 dollars an hour, drive to their patient's home, get little or no mileage reimbursement, and no compensation for completing a pile of paperwork, or, they could work in an outpatient setting in a clinic or hospital for decent money, not need to travel to each patient's home—and also have a lot less paperwork to process. It's no surprise that most licensed professionals chose outpatient work.

Of course, the licensing requirement was in part initiated by family advocates who were seeking better care for their kids with a diagnosis of a pervasive developmental disorder. But since BHRS services were 100 percent state-funded at that time, and clinical care for this population was expensive, the results didn't add up. This is one of the factors why parents—still—find it hard to find capable staff to help their families. No one will maintain these positions. Why would they? A shortage of qualified BSCs was inevitable, and that would make things even harder on families.

At The Stern Center, however, I was happy to discover I was able to put my "energy hat" back on. Carole, who is a licensed psychologist, in fact, trained others in Emotional Freedom Techniques (EFT), among many other energy techniques, so I was in good company. She gave me the green light to teach a little of it to the new staff and use it with the clients. For me, it was kind of a coming home to energy psychology in the treatment context.

* * * * *

At TSC, we learned that the prestigious Cleveland Clinic was setting up a program to treat people with spectrum disorders right down the street from our satellite office in Fayette County. The division of their children's hospital, Cleveland Clinic Autism Development Solutions (CCADS), established an affiliate relationship with the local hospital system, Highlands Hospital, to create what would be known as Highlands Hospital Regional Center for Autism (HHRCA). And I helped create the name! It was big news for the small community.

A co-worker told me that a director position was opening there that had my name all over it, but I wasn't sure I wanted to go for it. I wasn't unhappy at TSC, and I wasn't sure I wanted to make the leap again. I decided to accept the offer for an interview but didn't put much effort into preparing for it. I figured I had some unique ideas about treating pervasive developmental disorders, so they'd either love me or hate me.

Well, they loved me. My title would be Director of Autism Services, and my new job was two-fold. First, I was to act as both the principal and program director of HHRCA, a licensed private school. In the industry, we consider it a "center-based" facility as opposed to "community-based" because we were licensed as a private school, and students came to us. (However, the program did also include community integration as a holistic measure.) Second, I provided oversight to the HHRCA diagnostic center, which did full evaluations to determine if a child should be diagnosed as a pervasive developmental disorder or another mental health or behavioral issue. Evaluation day was dubbed "Baby Day;" we would evaluate children as young as months old. It should be noted that generally few if any of the diagnostic facilities in the Pittsburgh area would consider diagnosing a child under two years of age, but Cleveland Clinic Autism Development Solutions did. They had the most cutting-edge multi-disciplinary approach for doing so, and HHRCA would duplicate it.

I did my first two weeks of director training in Cleveland, Ohio, at Cleveland Clinic's Center for Autism, a division of their Children's Hospital. It was a school-based program, and it was the most amazing thing I'd ever seen. There were at least 100 students, many profoundly affected by the disorder, yet the classes and learning all seemed to go smoothly and seamlessly. The kids were sitting at desks, working on curriculum—even though many of them had hardly any verbal language skills. It was mind-blowing. The program provided curriculum and behavior management so that every kid there, no matter what their functioning levels were, could succeed and learn.

On my first day there, I was assigned to a CCADS consultant, Travis Haycook, my mentor at the clinic who was tasked with providing me with the tools to replicate the CCADS program from top to bottom. I took a clinical skills assessment screening exam devised by CCADS and scored very high on it. Out of curiosity, I asked Travis if he'd heard of energy psychology. He turned to me and said he thought that given my high test score, my biggest challenge with the program might be leaving behind anything that had to do with energy psychology. He told me their program adhered strictly to the treatment guidelines and methods of Applied Behavior Analysis (ABA). That wouldn't include EP.

ABA was and is the most well-researched and successful approach for treating children with pervasive developmental disorders. ABA interventions focus on improving specific behaviors such as social skills, communication, reading, and academics as well as adaptive learning skills, such as fine motor dexterity, grooming, domestic capabilities, punctuality, and job competence. In the 1990s, ABA facilities were emerging and gaining momentum in California, New Jersey, and Florida. At the time in Pennsylvania, some practices sent some of their therapists to the Lovaas Institute in California to get training in Discrete Trial Training (DTT), a structured ABA technique.

CCADS was taking steps to initiate affiliations with a few hospitals around the country and set up ABA-based programs to replicate their Center for Autism in Cleveland. Ours was the first one to complete the specs for affiliation with them, and it was my job to launch the Pittsburgh regional program. The design was exclusively ABA programming, which was fine with me at that point. After all, CCADS had the experts, they were getting progressive results, and I knew I still had a lot to learn about applied behavior analysis. After a couple of days in the training program, lightbulbs started going off in my head.

For so much of my career so far, when I watched my colleagues and trainers I'd have a million questions running around in my head about why they were using the methods they used. If I asked them, they wouldn't be able to answer, either; most were just doing what they were trained to do. But the Cleveland training, and Travis in particular, were finally giving me answers to my questions. They gave me insights into how their program ran and how they chose to make clinical decisions. All of my "why's" were finally getting explanations, and I realized that I had been asking the right questions for a very long time. Travis reinforced my thinking process, supported my "out of the box" thinking, and helped give me the momentum to continue on my unique career path.

The mastery I was gaining made me even more aware of the gaps in community-based services. Often schools were left with just two choices to deal with difficult kids on the autism spectrum: either send them to sensory rooms to chill out and do whatever they want or, if they're unmanageably aggressive, the school can send them out to residential programs. I rarely witnessed kids in schools actually receiving an education until I observed the Cleveland school program.

At HHRCA, I learned to administer the gold standard of autism diagnostic testing—the Autism Diagnostic Observation Schedule (ADOS) assessment—as well as the Autism Diagnostic Interview-Revised (ADI-R). Unlike other standard tests, these assessments are somewhat structured. They include specific questions for parents and caregivers, and they require a lot of direct interaction with the kid. They also demand clear, informed, and neutral judgment on the part of the administrator. These assessments made me appreciate the importance of what I'd learned about the psychological concept of "executive functioning," that I discuss in chapter two, and cognition as related to assessing behaviors. They help you recognize learning errors and cognition errors and the different ways that these kids think about things—in order for you to see why certain behaviors result.

Under the private school designation, I also received certification as a special ed teacher and as a school principal under a "social/emotional" category in education since they didn't have a category specifically for treatment of pervasive developmental disorders in private schools at that time. During my time there, I also obtained a certificate in autism education. California University of Pennsylvania had just begun to offer this advanced studies certification mostly for special education teachers to better support them with understanding and intervening with their students' ASD-related challenges. In addition to these certifications, I also took a year's worth of classes through the University of South Florida in Children's Mental Health Administration, which also brought to light many of the strengths and challenges of Pennsylvania's existing systems of care.

Back in Pennsylvania, our center got its license as a private school and became very successful. In addition to the full-time curriculum, students received speech therapy, occupational therapy, and physical therapy if they required it. Just like Cleveland's school, ours was a year-round program. We also extended support for students well beyond just the walls of the school. We knew that community interaction and social interaction would also be critically important, so we taught some parents how to do some interventions, too, and created individualized, community-based plans and pre-vocational goals for each student.

The people on my staff were great at their jobs. Most of them had a genuine desire to work with the kids and learned and adopted the skills I taught them. At the same time, I knew the quality of the training and supervision that would be required to get the program to excel, so I asked a lot of them. Their ability to be present and focused at all times was a necessity. After all, with this population, dangerous behaviors can erupt out of nowhere. Each staff person had to be able to pay close attention to each child they are working with to help shape their desired behaviors in order to reduce their maladaptive ones.

The truth is, it almost always takes painstaking repetition and reinforcement for children with this disorder to be able to change. And only one major behavior should be addressed at a time. Unfortunately, outsiders without an understanding of ABA sometimes accused it of being harsh. "After all, they're just kids," they'd say, implying that they should be treated with kid gloves and that we weren't taking a heart-centered approach. "But they're kids who need to learn to survive in the world," I'd tell them. "This is the only way to help them do that."

Then inspiration struck. I decided to introduce the staff to energy psychology so they *themselves* could benefit from it. Most seemed to resonate with the concepts, and many were able to apply some of the new techniques I taught them during and after the workday. The tools started to help our staff stay energized, feel more centered, and sometimes—when things got intense and exhausting—it even helped them continue to be functional and effective. Once again, energy psychology proved to be a profoundly valuable addition to the staff's set of tools.

Aside from all of the progress the children made, I also began to recognize that the health of the *caregiver* is extraordinarily important when it comes to succeeding with a child who is on the autism spectrum. The healthier they are, the more effective they'll be and the longer they'll be around to *be* a caregiver. Their good health is essential to the whole puzzle.

◆ ◆ ◆ ◆ ◆

In 2015, I received my professional counselor license, and I felt I could make a bigger difference by bringing together Applied Behavior Analysis methods and energy psychology tools in an outpatient setting where I could help both kids and parents. Unlike the residential and school-based work I'd done up until then, in an outpatient setting I could work with parents and caregivers and continue the coaching I had done in the school's community. I also knew that parents would seek me out for my expertise. I decided to develop a package consisting of ABA skills for managing the children plus techniques to use to manage their own stress. Once I started to meet with them, they would see the value and the power of the tools for themselves.

When I launched my outpatient practice, a customer service rep for one of the major insurance companies told me that they only had three outpatient therapists who specifically work with spectrum disorders in the whole Pittsburgh region. It was another testament to the gap in accessibility to services for the population. It was an echo of the misperception that I'd continue to hear for years: that doing outpatient work isn't effective or isn't possible with this population. The truth is, it's doable—you just have to be super knowledgeable and creative in order to get meaningful results and real change. You have to appreciate what makes those with ASD unique and recognize that caregiving for them is different, too. Most of all, you have to embrace the idea that the biggest changes start with you, the caregiver.

2

What's Going On with My Kid?

W hat *is* autism? Or autism spectrum disorder? Are there neurological or genetic conditions that factor into the way that
those diagnosed with it act, behave, think or feel? Let's take
a closer look, sort out the facts from the fiction, and get as clear a grasp
of the condition as we can. Knowledge is power; being informed about
the current scientific understanding of this population should empower
you tremendously as a caregiver.

To begin, let's be honest. While ASD has gained a great deal of
recognition over the last several decades, there is still a tremendous
amount of confusion and misinformation about it. In fact, even the
innumerable assessments and efforts to diagnose these disorders have
added to the muddle. Assessments rely on the assessors' observations
and conclusions about the presenting behaviors and turn out to be quite
subjective. Testing for genetic factors doesn't help simplify or clarify
things either; there's a great deal of variation in genetic testing results.
I had always been curious to know this: If a large sample of people who
have never been formally diagnosed with autism spectrum disorder
underwent the same genetic analysis that ASD-diagnosed people go
through, how much variation and how many surprises would we find?
I figured there is probably a tremendous overlap between populations.
We will look into a current answer to this later in the text. There's
rarely a cut-and-dried diagnosis.

To understand this diagnostic category, let's go back and review the
evolution of terms as defined by the American Psychiatric Association
(APA). In the first and second editions of the *Diagnostic & Statistical*

Manual (DSM)[4], the word "autism" was only connected to the presentation of childhood schizophrenia. It was not until the third edition, the DSM-III, published in 1980, that they first established autism as a separate diagnosis, called "infantile autism," which was listed completely separately from schizophrenia. Six criteria were required to be present before 30 months of age for the diagnosis to apply. In 1987 with the DSM-IIIR, the title was changed to "autistic disorder," and it was described as generally having a lack of response to others.

The APA didn't define autism as a "spectrum" of conditions until 1994, when it published its fourth edition, the DSM-IV. In that edition, "autism" was described as a complex developmental disorder that can cause problems with thinking, feeling, language, and the ability to relate to others. The DSM-IV characterized the disorder as consisting of three main categories: communication problems, difficulty relating to others, and repetitive body movements and behaviors, and each of the categories has several subcategories.

Communication problems can include, but are not limited to, difficulty using or understanding language, difficulty having a conversation beyond a very limited set of topics, repeating phrases frequently, and having very little vocal speech. Difficulties relating to people, things, and events can include, but are not limited to, challenges making friends and interacting with people, struggles with reading people's facial expressions, and—one of the most common assumptions about it—difficulties with making eye contact. Examples of repetitive body movements or behaviors are hand-flapping and repeating sounds or phrases, to name a few. This is not an exhaustive list of problems and challenges by any means. Everyone presents symptoms very differently.

But with the publication of the DSM-IV in 1994, there was a sea change in the definitions. As I mentioned in the last chapter, the DSM-IV had employed an umbrella category for autistic disorders— pervasive developmental disorders (PDD)—which included five diagnoses: autistic disorder, Rhett's disorder, childhood disintegrative

---

4 The DSM is the standard guideline that doctors, mental health professionals, and clinicians use when they're assessing and diagnosing mental health issues.

disorder, pervasive developmental disorder not otherwise specified, and Asperger's disorder. Then, in 2013, with the publication of the DSM-V, the APA scrapped that and created a new single diagnostic category—autism spectrum disorder. The new category included "spectrum" in its name in recognition that while those who have the condition can have certain symptoms in common, the intensity and severity of them can vary widely. To give practitioners the ability to convey the severity of the symptoms in a patient's diagnosis, the DSM defines three levels. Level 1 indicates "requiring support," Level 2 indicates "requiring substantial support," and Level 3 means "requiring very substantial support"—the most severe level of symptoms. So, for example, a formal diagnosis would be written as: "autism spectrum disorder, level 3, requiring very substantial support."

Unfortunately, the switch to the new diagnostic definitions of the DSM-V didn't eliminate all of the confusion. Many obsolete and more rigid, less fluid definitions can be problematic. For example, even though Asperger's disorder is no longer a diagnosis according to the DSM-V, it still remains in the vernacular; people seem to continue to just hand it down. This statement is not to be confused with those who formally met the criteria at the time of their diagnosis, when that particular diagnosis was contained in the current DSM. Another term that is still in circulation is "high functioning autism," which also has no meaning and can do more harm than good. For example, I've heard too many parents, when they reveal that their child has been diagnosed with "Asperger's," follow it immediately with: "He's high functioning!" But this is inaccurate and misleading as well as unfortunate.

Unfortunately, the switch to the new diagnostic definitions of the DSM-V didn't eliminate all of the confusion. Many obsolete and more rigid, less fluid definitions can be problematic. For example, even though Asperger's disorder is no longer a diagnosis according to the DSM-V, it still remains in the vernacular; people seem to continue to just hand it down. This statement is not to be confused with those who formally met the criteria at the time of their diagnosis, when that particular diagnosis was contained in the current DSM. Another term that is still in circulation is "high functioning autism," which also has no meaning and can do more harm than good. For example, I've heard too many parents, when they reveal that their child has been diagnosed with "Asperger's," follow it immediately with: "He's high functioning!" But this is inaccurate and misleading as well as unfortunate.

Here's why. Saying that a child is "high functioning" relies on a bunch of erroneous assumptions that ultimately cause more problems. By using that term, parents convince themselves that their child has some sort of a "higher" skill set—when that's not necessarily the case. Some diagnosticians use this term to soften the languaging when giving a diagnosis thinking it helps parents to minimize the child's condition as they think, "Oh, it's not that bad." Then they tell themselves their child can just get by with minimal intervention, and so they sometimes fail to ensure the kid gets the appropriate level of intervention that they need to function and interact more effectively in the world. Making matters worse, the child often feels stereotyped by the label and feels the pressure of being expected to function at a level that is beyond their capabilities. Being good at school does not necessarily predict success in all life domains in the future. Good parenting and good health means examining and providing support in all areas of a child's life.

Blanket statements about a diagnosis, too, can lead to overlooking some of the less obvious challenges the child is having. For example, even though kids diagnosed with Asperger's were able to demonstrate decent language skills and engage in reciprocity fairly well, they still had significant deficits in some of the more subtle aspects of social communication—aspects that are building blocks of success. If those are overlooked, it is a disservice to the child's development.

The more fluid definition of autism spectrum disorder offered by the DSM-V and the opportunity for the diagnosis to also communicate the level of support needed provides a much more realistic perspective of the disorder. It helps to remind us that each of the diagnoses shares a set of potential issues, yet that the degree to which each of those issues affects the individual will be unique to each person.

Neurological Differences

Now, beyond these psychological definitions, it's important to recognize that ASD is a neurological disorder since it affects the functioning of the brain. Physiologically, research has uncovered differences in the brain structure of those with ASD, and learning about them helps to bring more light to the topic, especially to those who interact with and care for those diagnosed with the disorder. These insights might be especially helpful when you find yourself wondering: "Why can't he just [*fill in the blank*] like other kids?" So, let's take a look at some of the research. While some of the information below can get a bit technical, it's worth getting familiar with it.

Most of the recent research agrees that there are abnormalities in the white and gray matter organization of the brain along with differences in cortex regions among those diagnosed with ASD when compared with those who are not. The research is complicated and continues to emerge.

Greimel, et al. indicate that "ASD is characterized by complex changes in gray matter developmental trajectories of several brain regions. These brain regions belong to neural networks that underpin social-cognitive and motor functions previously demonstrated to be impaired in ASD. Changes in gray matter development present during childhood and persisting into adolescence and adulthood are likely to contribute to social-cognitive and motor impairments in individuals affected by ASD."[5]

According to Greimel, compared to controls, ASD subjects showed reduced grey matter volumes in the anterior cingulate cortex, posterior superior temporal sulcus, and middle temporal gyrus. The anterior cingulate cortex is associated with higher-order social-emotional and cognitive functions, such as response monitoring and affective regulation. The posterior superior temporal sulcus and middle temporal gyrus play a role in social cognition and Theory of Mind.

The team also investigated age effects in the gray matter in their study

---

5 Greimel, E., Nehrkorn, B., Schulte-Ruther, M., Fink, G. R., Nickl-Jockschat, T., Herpertz-Dahlmann, B., Konrad, K. & Eickhoff, S. B. (2013). Changes in grey matter development in autism spectrum disorder. *Brain Structure and Function, 218*, 929–942.

which had a large sample size. This helped to resolve the inconclusive findings from previous studies in ASD. They write: "Results on age-related changes of regional gray matter volumes suggest that ASD is characterized by complex alterations in lifetime trajectories of several brain regions that underpin social-cognitive and motor functions." In the ASD group, age-related changes of gray matter volume in the amygdala, temporoparietal junction, septal nucleus, middle cingulate cortex, and precentral gyrus differed from controls."

MRIs and the Future of Assessment and Treatment

There's also exciting news on the technological front. Research using magnetic resonance imaging (MRI) has provided fascinating correlations between the structural differences in the brain and behavioral challenges, indicating that imaging might be able to play a valuable role in assessment and diagnosis of ASD in the future.

With increasing technology, researchers have been able to identify structural differences in the ASD brain. Meaning, the physical features of the ASD brain are different than a person who does not have ASD. Think about how this could affect the way we behave and understand the world. This is what we see in those diagnosed.

In his 2012 article, *Functional Magnetic Resonance Imaging of Autism Spectrum Disorders*, Gabriel Dichter, Ph.D., reported on his findings from doing functional magnetic resonance imaging (FMRIs) on people with autism spectrum disorders.[6] He described neurological differences in the subjects, including reduced activity in certain parts of the brain, unusual activity during some cognitive tasks, differences in the way language is processed, less-than-average communication between parts of the brain at times, and more. These are broad-brush descriptions, though; how they might pile up and/or interact in each person will be very individualized.

Dichter also emphasizes that each ASD-diagnosed person is unique—that his findings revealed common themes despite the "highly

---

6 Dichter, Gabriel S. "Functional magnetic resonance imaging of autism spectrum disorders." *Dialogues in clinical neuroscience* vol. 14,3 (2012): 319–51. doi:10.31887/DCNS.2012.14.3/gdichter

heterogeneous nature of ASDs." It's an important reminder to all of us that, for this population, the types of challenges, the severity of symptoms, and the resulting behaviors will always be unique to each person.

Even more interesting is that researchers are also starting to be able to correlate specific differences in the brain to behavioral demonstrations.

In European Psychiatry, Yvonne Schröder and her team demonstrate that "individuals with higher levels of autism-spectrum-like features show decreased white matter integrity in tracts associated with higher-level visual processing and increased cortical volume in areas linked to movement sequencing and working memory."[7]

Merel C. Postema's 2019 study examined brain symmetry in ASD with one of the largest sample sizes to date. Although these researchers caution using their findings solely as predictors of ASD, noteworthy differences in the ASD brain versus the non-ASD brain were found:

"ASD was significantly associated with alterations of cortical thickness asymmetry in mostly medial frontal, orbitofrontal, cingulate and inferior temporal areas, and also with asymmetry of orbitofrontal surface area. These differences generally involved reduced asymmetry in individuals with ASD compared to controls. Furthermore, putamen volume asymmetry was significantly increased in ASD."

Further: "The magnitude of all regional thickness asymmetries was decreased in ASD compared with controls, whether it was reduced leftward, reduced rightward, or reversed average asymmetry. Rightward asymmetry of the medial orbitofrontal surface area was also decreased in individuals with ASD, as was leftward asymmetry of the lateral orbitofrontal surface area. In addition, individuals with ASD showed an increase in leftward asymmetry of putamen volume, compared with controls."[8]

---

7 Schröder, Y., Hohmann, D. M., Meller, T., Evermann, U., Pfarr, J. K., Jansen, A., Kamp-Becker, I., Grezellschak, S., & Nenadić, I. (2021). Associations of subclinical autistic-like traits with brain structural variation using diffusion tensor imaging and voxel-based morphometry. European *Psychiatry: the journal of the Association of European Psychiatrists, 64*(1), e27. https://doi.org/10.1192/j.eurpsy.2021.15

8 Postema, M. C., van Rooij, D., Anagnostou, E., Arango, C., Auzias, G., Behrmann, M., Filho, G. B., Calderoni, S., Calvo, R., Daly, E., Deruelle, C., Di Martino, A., Dinstein, I., Duran, F., Durston, S., Ecker, C., Ehrlich, S., Fair, D., Fedor, J., Feng, X., Francks, C. (2019). Altered structural brain asymmetry in autism spectrum disorder in a study of 54 datasets. *Nature communications, 10*(1), 4958. https://doi.org/10.1038/s41467-019-13005-8

However, other scientists are researching with the intention of being able to predict ASD by scans. Think about being able to predict what ASD behaviors a person might exhibit by scanning their brains!

According to a study by the Radiological Society of North America and led by Julia P. Owen, a brain researcher at the University of Washington in Seattle, researchers using MRI technology identified structural abnormalities in the brains of people with one of the most common genetic causes of spectrum disorders—abnormalities in the 16th chromosome of the DNA strand.[9] And these abnormalities also corresponded to cognitive-behavioral impairments.

According to the study, many people on the autism spectrum have an unusually high number of abnormalities in the 16th chromosome, and when those abnormalities are present, certain behaviors have more potential to manifest. Thus, these abnormalities are considered some of the common genetic causes of autism spectrum disorder. The use of MRIs, then, allowed the researchers to identify which areas of cognitive deficits the ASD participant had and predict the kinds of difficulties they would experience.

The genetic brain abnormalities consisted primarily of two things: "deletions," meaning a small piece of the chromosome is lost, and "duplications," meaning a section is repeated. Physiologically, the study found that people with deletions tend to have brain overgrowth, and behaviorally, they tend to have developmental delays and a higher risk of obesity. Those with chromosomal duplication are born with smaller brains and tend to have lower body weight and developmental delays, according to the research. The study also found that the corpus callosum—the fiber bundle that connects the left and right sides of the brain—was abnormally shaped and thicker in those with chromosomal deletions but thinner in those with chromosomal duplication compared to the control group.

Beyond these findings, with the help of MRIs, researchers were also able to make correlations between abnormalities in the brain and behav-

---

9 *Brain MR Imaging Findings and Associated Outcomes in Carriers of the Reciprocal Copy Number Variation at 16p11.2* Julia P. Owen, Polina Bukshpun, Nicholas Pojman, Tony Thieu, Qixuan Chen, Jihui Lee, Debra D'Angelo, Orit A. Glenn, Jill V. Hunter, Jeffrey I. Berman, Timothy P. Roberts, Randy Buckner, Srikantan S. Nagarajan, Pratik Mukherjee, and Elliott H. Sherr. Radiology 2018 286:1, 217–226

ioral deficits with pretty impressive accuracy. Abnormalities were seen on brain images corresponding to both cognitive and behavioral impairments in the study group.

I had the privilege of Dr. Caleb Bupp accepting my request to contribute the following short essay about genetic testing. He is a medical genetics physician and Division Chief of Medical Genetics and Genomics at Corewell Health and Helen DeVos Children's Hospital in Grand Rapids, Michigan.

> The understanding of genetics has helped provide additional answers and clarity about autism. It was not until the mid 1950s that we accurately knew a human had 46 chromosomes, and now we are able to sequence the billions of nucleotides in a person's genome. The Human Genome Project, completed nearly 25 years ago, took over a decade to complete at the cost of $2.7 billion, and now a genome can be sequenced in hours at a cost of nearly a thousand dollars. Advances in technology have made this all possible, and this has accelerated genetic diagnosis tremendously. Genetic testing is now readily available and able to be deployed to diagnose patients and inform medical management.
>
> Genetic testing and diagnoses can help understand the diagnosis of autism. Identifying a patient's genetic syndrome cannot remove the diagnosis of autism, and genetic testing itself cannot diagnose autism. Finding out someone has something like Down syndrome or Fragile X syndrome can help clarify why the person has autism. There are now hundreds to thousands of different genetic diagnoses that have autism as a feature. Broad genetic testing like chromosome microarray, whole exome sequencing, and whole genome sequencing allow an individual to have their genetic code scanned for millions of different genetic changes with one single test.
>
> Genetic testing does come with risks. The main ones are the chance of finding something unexpected or something uncertain. Unexpected results can include genetic changes that impact a person's health in ways unrelated to why the testing was performed. In cases of autism, patients may be informed they have a mutation in the *BRCA1* or *BRCA2* gene which predis-

poses an individual to be diagnosed with breast, ovarian, and other cancers.

It is unlikely why the testing was done but this information is now known after testing is done. This can translate to improved care, such as early screening for cancer, but it also may impair someone's ability to get life insurance, disability insurance, and long-term care insurance because there are not protections in place against discrimination based on genetic information. Uncertain results from the testing are also possible, which are changes in the genetic code that are not clearly understood and might be the answer to the diagnosis of a patient's illness or completely unimportant information.

For individuals with autism, genetic counseling and genetic testing should always be offered and considered. This does not mean that each person should have testing, since it is a very personal decision that must be made by each individual and family. There is great power in finding a genetic diagnosis answer for a person with autism, such as relieving guilt, helping with access to services and interventions, connecting with communities of others who have the same diagnosis, advancing research, and providing guidance for other medical concerns that may come with the genetic diagnosis. Understanding these benefits along with the potential risks is important for making an informed decision that is truly right for each patient and family .

Caleb Bupp, MD, FACMG, is a pediatrics trained, board-certified medical geneticist with Corewell Health and Helen DeVos Children's Hospital in Grand Rapids, Michigan. He serves as the Division Chief of Medical Genetics and Genomics. He is also an assistant professor at Michigan State University.

Dr. Bupp received his Bachelor of Science in molecular biology from Grove City College in Grove City, Pennsylvania and his medical degree from the University of Toledo College of Medicine in Ohio. He completed pediatrics residency at the University of Louisville in Kentucky and his medical genetics training at the Greenwood Genetic Center in South Carolina.

He co-discovered a treatable genetic syndrome caused by ODC1 mutations now termed Bachmann-Bupp syndrome and is the clinical director of the International Center for Polyamine Disorders. He helped create and run Project Baby Deer, a statewide initiative to provide access to rapid whole genome sequencing which resulted in Michigan Medicaid being the first to create an approval and carve-out payment policy. Dr. Bupp helped form the Rare Disease Network which provides support and education throughout Michigan.

Technological developments like these are very exciting and might very well turn out to be extremely helpful for diagnosis and, ultimately, treatment. I'm hoping that we see a lot more research like it in the future. If MRIs and genetics can reveal to us the specific cognitive and learning difficulties that ASD-diagnosed kids have, it might reduce the amount of work needed to accomplish accurate assessments and effective treatment plans. We might be able to save a tremendous amount of time as we try to assess cognitive processes known as executive functioning capabilities, which, in turn, help us help those on the spectrum to live more comfortably in the world.

Executive Functioning Skills

When we work with the ASD population, it's simply essential that we put ourselves in their shoes—and even in their heads—to better understand what gets them upset, getting them to go from zero to sixty in five seconds sometimes. The truth is that, in general, those on the spectrum usually orient themselves in the world through "recipes" or formulas for success. And while every kid is unique. Each kid is somewhat uniquely predictable in the way that their mind will formulate processes into repeatable recipes. That means that, to some degree, we can anticipate how they think and where breakdowns in their processing of information might occur. Understanding the mind's executive functioning skills helps us do that.

For decades, treatment of young people on the autism spectrum focused predominantly on observing behavior and then asking the child "Why" questions. The well-intended caregiver or professional would ask, "Why did you . . .?" or "Why are you . . .?" or "Why does . . .?" over and over again. Understandably, these questions typically come from a traditional therapeutic orientation. But the truth is, the responses to these questions can often come loaded with a certain amount of anger or frustration. Yet, some insights can still be gained in the process. For example, we might hear: "He wouldn't let me . . ." and we might learn something about where the child's needs aren't being met. In the bigger picture, however, these basic questions often aren't enough to facilitate behavior change. Caregivers are often at a loss about how to get underneath the sudden upsets, the tantrums, the oppositional behavior, or whatever. These questions only get them so far.

If we only have a short list of questions to ask, we're just not going to get very far when we want to get inside a kid's head and get a better understanding of what's really happening for them. In addition, if the answers we get aren't insightful enough, we might try to figure things out ourselves. Unfortunately, when we do that, it's incredibly easy (and human nature!) to project onto them our own ideas of why they do what they do based on what we've seen in others or ourselves. Maybe we've seen similar behavior from other kids and think the same motivation applies, or maybe we conclude that's how we would think or feel in the situation, and we assume the kid would feel the same way. But we're guessing, and we're often wrong. Without a way to more effectively investigate what's going on with them, we have a very frustrating experience on our hands.

Learning the basics of how the mind's executive functioning skills work can help give caregivers a deeper grasp of what is fueling the maladaptive behaviors they're witnessing. It can also help them become more effective at caregiving as well as actually seeing behaviors improve.

What are these skills? They are a collection of cognitive functions all of us use all the time to help us process information and manage life tasks of all types. These cognitive skills are what allow us to pay attention, organize, plan, begin and follow through on tasks, and more. The prefrontal cortex, located in the front of the brain, is responsible for our executive functioning processes. While some sources cite more, I find it best to focus on seven general categories of executive functioning skills:

- Inhibition
- Flexibility
- Attention

- Memory
- Planning
- Problem solving
- Metacognition

As important as these abilities are, most of us take them for granted most of the time.

Being familiar with these executive functions can come in very handy to caregivers at those times when an ASD-diagnosed kid is confronted by a somewhat challenging task, so they become heightened or escalated because of it. Being familiar with them helps us notice an area to troubleshoot before they reach a threshold of some sort. Then we can stop and ask much better, more specific questions than just "Why did you do that?" and get more meaningful answers. We can begin to investigate where the breakdown happened and what preceded it. With that information, we can establish some targeted retraining that helps avoid occurrences of similar outbursts from happening in the future.

Let's take a close look at the seven categories of executive functioning:

> **Inhibition.** We need the skill of inhibition to be able to wait our turn, whether at the grocery line or in a conversation. In fact, when kids go to school, this executive function is hammered home as we teach them to wait their turn, hold their tongue, or not pick up their pencil until directed, for example. Without even realizing it, most of us make countless decisions each day pertaining to how long we should wait to do something. For kids in school settings, for example, the skill is called into play when students ask themselves: *When is it OK to pick up my pencil? When do I need to pick it up? When do I need to wait? When can I raise my hand? When do I need to put my hand down? When can I speak? When shouldn't I speak?*

> **Flexibility.** How well can you switch to another topic when a new one is brought up? How well can you change gears, and how quickly can you accommodate new information? These skills have to do with the executive function of flexibility, also sometimes also called "set shifting." It mostly has to do with how we

transition from one thing to the next and how quickly and appropriately we can adapt our thinking to changing circumstances.

Attention. We all seem to assume we know what attention is, but do we really? Joint attention, in particular—being able to coordinate one's focus of attention with another person— does not necessarily mean only using words. Attention can be really tough for a lot of older kids with ASD, especially when it comes to higher-level problem-solving skills in reading, language arts, and math. It requires being able to sustain, divide, and alternate one's attention effectively. We're doing this when we're in the workplace; we are listening and determining relevance and saliency, as in the questions: What's important? What should I pick out to focus on? And when?

Conversational attention can be an incredibly complex task if you think about it. For example, if a person is listening to someone and wants to be engaged in the topic of conversation, they have to take the words in, comprehend the words, and then attach some meaning to them based on their own life experience. Then they consider what kind of response they want to make and begin to formulate their response in a way that relates to the topic and to the other. Then they have to wait for a break in the conversation—with the help of the inhibition executive function, of course—for an opportunity to respond. Finally, they can articulate their response. If all cylinders are running, all of this happens in the blink of an eye. Yet, it can be incredibly challenging for those diagnosed with ASD.

A component of attention is saliency, which, for the purpose of this discussion, is the ability to pick out what's most important in a task or in written or spoken communication. The question is: *What stands out?* Saliency also requires some knowledge of the context around the item. It is a somewhat advanced skill for those on the spectrum and one that is often overlooked, especially when parents or professionals oversimplify by using terms like "high functioning." A kid might be very good at many other things but struggle a lot with the ability to tease out what is important, especially in social situations. It is a key tool in life.

Inattention and planning, which I discuss below, are common in the ASD population. Unfortunately, these days, when behaviors that seem to appear to be inattention are noticed, kids often end up being given a co-diagnosis of ADHD to explain it. But behaviors that appear to be attention-deficit-related can stem from a combination of errors in both attention and planning executive functions. Of course, sometimes, a diagnosis of ADHD is clinically warranted. However, there are many ways of diagnosing executive functioning errors in order to correct the skill deficit.

If attention skills and memory skills are parcellated, it can be even more challenging for the ASD population. They'll experience more processing errors and ultimately feel especially overloaded.

Memory. Another vital component of executive functioning is memory. Memory can be categorized into several types, including associative, visual, spatial, auditory, episodic, and working memory. Working memory is especially relevant to this discussion because it allows us to hold different chunks of information in our minds at the same time, encode them somehow, and be able to recall them—even while we're doing something else. Kids need a functioning working memory when they're doing school tasks. But having a good working memory is especially challenging for the ASD population; I consistently see a lot of errors when it's called for in those I work with.

Planning. When the ASD-diagnosed are trying to plan, they often have difficulty, whether they're trying to plan a task, plan a social experience, set goals, create a plan for initiating tasks, or even monitor their progress as they try to accomplish something. Time management can be a challenge for ASD-diagnosed kids, and they can struggle with using a planner, self-organization, and thinking ahead Planning often goes hand in hand with attention skills.

Problem solving. Most of us do a lot more problem solving than we realize. A lot of my work with the ASD population is around trying to help them improve their problem-solving skills. There's non-social problem solving, which, in a school setting, can include things like higher-level math problems or even trying to navigate one's way through academics. Non-social problem-solving questions kids might ask themselves include: What do I do next? What do I need for my next class? And Can I go to my locker? Social problem-solving questions include: How do I react to what a person says to me? How do I react to a person after I respond? Do I turn and walk away? Do I say something back? Do I just make a facial expression or a gesture?? What do I do?

Metacognition. Metacognition requires putting together all the other pieces of executive functioning. It has to do with our ability to monitor ourselves, the act of thinking about our own thinking. That's what's in play when we ask ourselves questions like: *How do I think as compared to how others think? Do others have opinions that are different than mine? Are my learning strategies working for me?*

Metacognition acts as the gatekeeper for most of the other executive functioning skills, and for any of us to master it, all of the other types of executive functioning must be working well. In other words, if one of the other dominoes falls, metacognition will also fall along with it.

Almost all ASD-diagnosed kids seem to need some assistance with metacognitive functioning at some point. (However, that's not to say that other young people don't also need some coaching on it, too! It's a tough one to master.)

◆ ◆ ◆ ◆ ◆

Those diagnosed with autism spectrum disorder can, in part, be defined by the presence of errors in their executive functioning skills. In fact, the structural and neurological differences described earlier have a huge impact on the executive functions—and malfunctions—that people experience. They are integral to the ASD condition in that they underly the vast majority of their behaviors. (Again, the rest of the population has them too, but not to the same extent.) These disruptive learning errors get in the way of their ability to process information and impulses gracefully or appropriately—and that, in turn, can become extremely frustrating to them. The frustration itself can compound maladaptive behaviors. Complicating matters further, several malfunctions can pile on top of each other, fueling upsets and making it even more challenging for caregivers to figure out what's happening and what set them off.

Kids that are more profoundly affected can have multiple errors happening all the time.

People can experience executive function errors in different ways. Sometimes it's a feeling like something "doesn't compute." Sometimes people mistakenly jump over a task in the sequence and quickly start to feel stymied. Sometimes people tell me, "Oh, something else popped in my head," disrupting their process.

Once we're clued in about the mind's executive functions, we understand more about how the brain processes information and tasks, which leads to more precise insights about autism spectrum disorder behaviors. That helps us avoid those seductive rabbit holes—repeatedly asking those unfruitful questions—that often end up creating *more* upset and resentment rather than reducing them.

Here's an example. I was in a session with a teenager diagnosed with ASD; he was a young man that some people liked to describe as "high functioning," and some people questioned if he really had a spectrum disorder. His mom began the session by turning to him and, slowly and calmly, tried explaining the issue to him. Her intentions were great, and she wanted to be clear and specific, so she continued to share detail after detail. After a short time, the young man all of a sudden bursts out his feelings. He was very agitated, and said, "I don't know what you're saying! Stop yelling at me!" His mom, of course, defended herself, saying, "I'm just trying to explain this to you, so you'll understand."

But I saw it coming. I could observe where glitches in his executive functioning were creating havoc for him. It seemed to me he had hinged on to the first couple of things she had articulated, but he also was well aware of the social etiquette "recipe" that he had been taught—that he shouldn't barge into a conversation impulsively. He should wait for his turn. His inhibitive executive functioning skills were doing their job.

But as he held the information in, it became too much for him to hold on to his response while also continuing to receive even more information from her. He wasn't able to hold attention well—to listen and register the information (encode) at the same time. He lost the ability to keep attention because he was trying to formulate his own thoughts and was focused on that. We know that, as a rule, when any of the other six executive functions fail, the metacognitive function soon falls away, too. Sure enough, his metacognitive skills glitched, and he wasn't aware of how he was reacting to her long explanation. Then what happened? Difficult behavior. His frustration rose, his impulsivity kicked in, and the dam just broke. And out came—well, whatever—from his mouth.

His mom had been doing her best, but as she continued, I could tell by his bodily clues—he was looking down and sometimes looking away—that he was reaching the limits of his capacity to absorb what she was saying. It was becoming too much information for him to take in all at once. So while she understandably wanted to be heard and wanted to finish her thought, the teenager had reached his threshold.

Once I saw how the young man's mind was having trouble processing information, I knew I'd want to speak to him with smaller chunks of information from then on and check in with him along the way about how well he was processing it.

Reading behavioral cues like this can guide us to ask better and more productive questions. The answers to those questions then help us anticipate where kids might get confused—where the errors might occur—in the future, and we can begin error remediation beforehand. We can also help them develop skills to navigate their lives easier, knowing that the glitches will most likely continue to occur. I'll go more in-depth about reading behavioral cues in the next chapter. Sometimes we caregivers simply get overfocused on teaching emotional regulation for this group of kids because we feel bad about them being upset. But in my experience, more often than not, working with errors in executive functioning is the key to disengaging many of the emotional dysregulation issues in this population.

Knowing about the mind's executive functions helps us ask better questions, which in turn helps us come up with better treatment solutions. We can say, "Tell me more." Instead of asking general "why" questions without context, we can inquire: "You wanted to listen, but you couldn't wait for her to finish. Why couldn't you wait?" And if he answers, "It just happened so fast, I couldn't stop it," immediately we'd know that the escalation was a result of the inhibition error there, and we can respond to that specifically. We can ask more questions than just "Why" and begin to line up the whole entire thought process they go through. Some kids can't even give an answer to "Why," so we might need to break down the questions in different ways. The more that we do that, the more we can put the pieces together about how each person is programmed. Then things get easier. I'll say more about asking better questions in chapter four.

We don't have to be hyper-focused on behaviors and emotional regulation anymore, as we were trained to do as behaviorists. We don't have to analyze every single one to make progress. We can focus more on the process and find out where the glitches are happening, glitches that fuel the behavior.

If their tools are ineffective tools, caregivers will find themselves having to put out fires as they react to all sorts of maladaptive behaviors. But with better tools in hand, such as knowing the way the mind functions and knowing how to ask better questions, there are fewer fires to put out, and there's more time to enjoy each other's company.

People with autism spectrum disorder often find that formulas are their best friends. Formulas are the lens through which they see life, make decisions, and, often, communicate. They are known quantities. So to help them navigate an inhospitable and variegated world, they will store formulas in their minds that they can access them when in unfamiliar or questionable environments or situations. Formulas give them a better chance of responding to events in acceptable ways.

Formulas can consist of scripts or other memorized content, repeated phrases, and the like. If a child hears a monologue they like on TV, for example, they might memorize it and use it in a conversation when they experience a gap. Then, if someone asks a question they don't have an answer to, they might respond with that monologue. They might pair the question with the words they like to say—and cut and paste it in to fill the gap—either because they think it might work or because it just provides comfort.

But life is often unpredictable, so when their formulas fail them, they often get upset and exhibit difficult behaviors. If they don't have the foundational skills of knowing how to recall what they know and apply it to, say, a social situation, then they react to the situation in often escalated ways. If they don't know what to do about a missing piece to their formula, they react.

◆ ◆ ◆ ◆ ◆

Our understanding of how the brains and minds of people with ASD function has come a long way in the past few decades and informs and empowers us to become more skilled at helping those we're caring for. The next step is to learn some of the extremely productive principles that make up the most commonly used intervention and treatment modality available today: Applied Behavior Analysis, or ABA.

3

Start with the ABCs

Applied Behavior Analysis (ABA) was one of the first modalities I learned about for treating people with an autism spectrum disorder. It is a type of therapy that focuses on changing specific behaviors—such as social skills, communication, reading, academics, and adaptive learning skills—by using reinforcement techniques. It is the single most well-researched and most commonly used intervention and treatment modality that professionals use to treat people with ASD. And it has a uniquely scientific approach to understanding behavior since it relies on objective information about behaviors to make treatment decisions.

Essentially, ABA applies respected behavioral principles to everyday situations to do two things: increase the number of adaptive, constructive behaviors expressed by a person with autism spectrum disorder and decrease the number of maladaptive behaviors. When it's done well, ABA also helps transfer skills and behaviors from one situation to another, based on a set of specific strategies that you use before problems arise and also after the problematic behaviors are evident. For young and old, ABA can help individuals manage some of the lifestyle challenges that accompany many mental and physical health issues that warrant improvement.

But while Applied Behavior Analysis is mostly discussed here pertaining to autism spectrum disorder, it can apply to all of us. It is concerned with what motivates us, what engages our behaviors, and what deters us from continuing behaviors. Many of us go to work, for example, because we're motivated in some way. Maybe we love our job, or maybe it provides us a certain kind of self-expression and satisfaction—all internal gratifications. But many of us might be motivated by the more tangible motivation of a paycheck or the things we can pay for with our paycheck. If we want to change almost any behavior that we engage in our lives, we can look at it through an ABA lens. This is why ABA has such great research behind it—it applies to just about everything we do. If we're able to pare down to the most elemental levels of what can help motivate someone to change, we're on to something for all of us.

I use ABA in couples counseling a lot, where, of course, people often want their spouse's behavior to change. And I'll tell them, "Okay, let's clarify what the undesired behavior is, and then we're going to look at what comes before it." We'll identify the behavior in one person and figure out what is the *antecedent*—the behavior in the other person that came before the behavior the partner wanted to change. If the antecedent changes, the responding behavior will usually change. And guess what. It works. And *everybody* feels better.

As a rule, when we use ABA to work with a kid diagnosed with autism spectrum disorder, we will pick one or two behaviors to change or one or two tasks to learn, and we'll start with the most significant one. We want to keep things simple. We start with small targets, and as we build success, we can group them into larger tasks over time.

Applied Behavior Analysis and Discrete Trial Training

There are many types of specific treatments that fall under the ABA umbrella, but I have traditionally focused on Discrete Trial Training (DTT) because it's the one I've used most widely—in modified forms—in school settings and in home practice when parents are trying to teach their children. In fact, it can be quite useful as a teaching tool for kids of all types—whether diagnosed with ASD or not. As a teaching strategy, DTT is all about breaking a task down into smaller, more teachable components and teaching each component separately. Prompting strategies, reinforcement strategies, and outcome-based decision-making play a big role in its success.

Very generally, Discrete Trial Training prescribes five steps to the process of encouraging or discouraging a behavior. The first is basically the directive or command, called a "discriminative stimulus." It is encouraged that the directive expresses the "three C's" of ABA: be clear, concise, and consistent. Being too wordy or giving multiple directives in one breath are common mistakes and can undercut all the rest of the efforts. What's most effective is a *directive* that's simple and to the point. The second step is a *response*. You either get the desired response or not. The third step is *prompting*, if necessary, and the fourth is the *consequence*—the form of reinforcement that will be delivered if earned, which I discuss below. Finally, the last step is the *period of time* after the consequence and before the next directive.

The ABCs of Applied Behavior Analysis

ABA uses an Antecedent-Behavior-Consequence (ABC) model. It helps us modify a behavior by looking at what comes right before it—the antecedent—and what comes immediately after—the *consequence*. It examines the behaviors we might want to change, the triggers behind those behaviors, and their impact on maladaptive patterns.

Antecedents might be things in the environment or social settings, topics of conversation, or even word choices. They are the triggering events. Antecedents can consist of things that happen and are observable right before the behavior presents itself. They can be accompanied by *setting events* or *slow triggers*. Both setting events and slow triggers can themselves serve as the antecedent.

It might take a little bit of research to uncover slow triggers. They can be thought of as background noise and might be present long before we see a maladaptive behavior. They can usually be found by examining the individual's behavioral history and physiological and environmental conditions. Slow triggers can be anything from the room temperature, a medication's side effects, the presence or absence of other people, or being in a crowd to something internal, such as a bellyache.

I've found that slow triggers are often underexamined in kids with ASD. This population can suffer from a variety of physical ailments—

from significant physical health issues with observable symptoms to other aliments where symptoms are not obvious—any of which can potentially affect their behavior. Parents sometimes start to piece together the puzzle of what is affecting their child. As you can see, determining antecedents to a problematic behavior takes lots of analysis and exploration. It's not always straightforward.

The *behavior*, of course, is just that—the targeted behavior or the behavior in question. In the context of the ASD-diagnosed population, we're usually talking about school-age kids' maladaptive behaviors, such as running outside the door, hitting the table with a fist, getting up from the dinner table without eating, yelling expletives, throwing paper on the floor, and kicking people. I'll talk in-depth about behaviors in the next chapter.

Consequences, then, are the resulting responses that are doled out immediately after a behavior. They play a big role in influencing whether the person chooses to continue a habitual behavior or not. When we work with the ASD population, we dole out consequences to help minimize troublesome behaviors or reward the behaviors we're trying to teach. In general, adaptive behaviors result in positive consequences, while maladaptive behaviors result in unpleasant consequences. But it can get more complicated than that, as you'll soon see. Consequences in everyday life can just be what happens immediately after a behavior. For example, I hand a cashier my credit card (behavior) they run it though a machine (consequence).

Consequences can be in the form of rewards that are earned or punishments that are deserved and given out immediately following the targeted behavior in order to see a change in behavior. As cognitive capacity grows and the child matures, we might be able to delay reinforcement somewhat, but for lasting results, we need to have a structured plan that we follow that will allow us to stretch out or delay reinforcement more and more over time.

For best results, consequences are well thought out in advance in a reinforcement plan that includes judgment calls about how reinforcement will consider the child's developmental level.

Prompts and Reinforcements

Most of the work I do with families and clients in an outpatient setting involves two teaching tools from discrete trial training: prompts and reinforcements. The use of prompts and reinforcements are incredibly helpful as we work to motivate kids to change and improve their behaviors and eliminate behaviors that are problematic.

Prompts are basically the help, support, or cues we give to help a child do something. When the child is given a gift, for example, the parent might give a verbal prompt such as "What do you say?" in the interest of having the child say, "Thank you." Other common verbal prompts are: "What happens now?" or "What do we do now?" The intention behind the verbal prompt is to help the child remember the next step or task in a series. For example, learning to tie a shoe takes several steps, and we want the child to learn the whole set of steps and complete the task. Ideally, we do our best to offer assistance consistently and reliably until the child does it right, completely on their own and without any of our prompts. We can prompt physically, too, by actually doing a task for the child, such as placing toothpaste on the toothbrush or washing their face.

Unfortunately, most of us are way too wordy when it comes to prompts. Verbal directives are one kind of prompt, and we often just try too hard to get it right and be specific: "Honey! Can you please, after you're done with this, take that outside? I need you to do that for me. Thank you." But what is that person really trying to say? Simply "Do this thing." Right? But we add filler words and ideas, which the autism spectrum disorder population often finds confusing and can't process very quickly. They have to navigate around all those extra words to mine the meaning we're offering them. We also often make the mistake of inserting "please" and "thank you," which aren't appropriate in situations when we're requiring them to do something.

Even with the best of intentions—trying to be helpful—it's easy to overdo it when it comes to prompting. For example, let's say little Jason says, "I don't want to brush my teeth, Mom. I don't want to learn how." The parent might put the toothpaste on the toothbrush—which is a prompt. In fact, if the parent comes into the bathroom and puts the toothpaste on the toothbrush—that's Prompt One. But Jason still doesn't follow through and brush his teeth. So, the parent holds the toothbrush up to the kid's mouth, which is Prompt Two. Then the parent actually starts brushing Jason's teeth. Prompt Three. Three intrusive prompts, just trying to get the kid to brush his teeth.

Way too many parents give prompts all day long—trying to do the right thing—without realizing what they're doing is not getting any closer to establishing their child's independence. Some parents just gamble on the idea that the kid will just do it someday. Even worse, these parents often recognize they are doing the task for the child and feel that there isn't much hope for the child to ever do it on their own.

The problem with overdoing prompting is that parents very often end up conditioning their kids to become prompt-dependent; this is significantly more likely when the kid is diagnosed with ASD. For one thing, it isn't easy for some of this population to tell you what they need or want. And secondly, the parent starts to anticipate their needs because they can see their behavior pattern coming, and they know what to do. It's just super easy to do it themselves, right? Unfortunately, it ends up being a factor in why the child doesn't make much progress with that skill. For the record, it's not only parents that make this mistake. Some behavior therapists and teaching staff do the same thing without realizing it.

For these reasons, it's important to set up a "prompt hierarchy" to reduce the intrusiveness and frequency of the prompts as much as possible. A prompt hierarchy generally refers to a process of moving from providing physical assistance to simply giving a subtle cue. The frequency of prompting simply has to decrease over time if the child is going to build a sense of independence. Yes, this approach does become very methodical, and it's up to the parent to do most of the work as usual—only they have to do it in a different way. Most parents need to work with a specialist to give them specific directions about how to work with prompting effectively.

Consequence Strategies: Reinforcement and Punishment

As I've mentioned, any event that follows as a result of a behavior is a consequence. Further, the strategies we put in place to address a behavior after it's happened are *consequence strategies*, and the most common of these are of a reinforcing or punishing nature. The definition of *reinforcement* is to maintain or increase the likelihood of the child repeating a desired behavior the same way with the same successful outcome in the future. *Reinforcers* are what we use to bolster the desired behavior. We want the learner to be motivated, and we're trying to move away from default verbal scolding like saying to a child, "No! That's bad!" mainly because it doesn't teach the correct behavior.

A *punishment*, on the other hand, is what we do to *decrease* the occurrence of a targeted behavior (which is usually not a desired behavior) in the future. When we think of punishment, most of us usually think of something physically hurtful, but by definition, and in this context, a punishment is any intervention designed to decrease a targeted behavior. Now here's where the language of our field can start to be confusing to lay people. Both reinforcements and punishments can be either "positive" or "negative," where "positive" simply means you're adding something and "negative" means you're removing something. Either way, the objective is to help motivate the young person to exhibit improved behavior. In the field of behavior modification, we have to set aside old assumptions that "positive" and "negative" mean "good" and "bad."

Let's look at some basic examples. If we know a child likes dessert and looks forward to having dessert after eating a nutritious dinner, we first have to define the targeted behavior or the goal. The goal is to have the kid eat the main meal. We want to increase the likelihood of him doing that, so we'd look for a reinforcement strategy. If he eats his dinner and gets the dessert that he really wants as a consequence, we have added an event to the experience and have therefore implemented a positive reinforcement strategy.

Most examples can be defined so that a reinforcement strategy is added. It is a matter of definition. On the other hand, if the child

	REINFORCEMENT	PUNISHMENT
Positive	ADD something to maintain or **increase** a behavior ⬆	ADD something to **reduce** or extinguish a behavior ⬇
Negative	REMOVE something to maintain or **increase** a behavior ⬆	REMOVE something to **reduce** or extinguish a behavior ⬇

has difficulty getting his homework done because of procrastination and hatred of chores, we can tell him that if he gets his homework done by 5:00 p.m., he is free of all chores for that evening. Taking away his chores is removing a non-preferred task (negative) to maintain or increase (reinforce) the child completing his homework early. It becomes a "negative" reinforcement strategy. You can see how these terms follow definitions and logic, not emotional judgments.

Now, which is better: reinforcement or punishment? Both reinforcement and punishment can be very effective, depending on what works for the child and what the targeted behavior is. When people who aren't experienced in behavior modification want to stop or reduce a behavior, chances are they'll opt for a punishment—something that will have a strong impact on the child. Or they will default to bribing the child. If they want to increase a behavior, they'll likely try a reinforcement strategy of some sort. This can get very complicated, and there are many choices the behavior specialist needs to make through a thorough assessment.

Doing this on your own without experience can be hit or miss. Most families I have worked with will say they have tried "rewards," but they don't work—either in the short term or in the long term. That is because there are many aspects that need to be considered, and they are highly individualized for the child. But the following will help give you some guidelines.

When using reinforcements or rewards in the beginning stages of treatment of those in the ASD population, we need to communicate them right after the targeted behavior happens so they can immediately associate one with the other. Basic guidelines are that reinforcement should be earned, it should be natural and age-appropriate, and what is offered for reinforcement should not be offered at other times in most cases.

Finally, reinforcements need to be constantly assessed to make sure they are still highly desired and that they are still working. Otherwise, they're of no use to you. Most of us don't like having the same things over and over again all the time. We get tired of the sameness. But ASD-diagnosed kids can go to extremes in either direction. Some consistently need new and different reinforcements, while others continue to get reinforcement value out of the same reinforcer for a very long time. Even if you think your child likes to stick with the same preferred items, you should frequently assess the reinforcements you're using.

Keep in mind that punishment can be quite effective, too, if used correctly. I've worked with informed and consenting adult individuals who were just not motivated enough by any potential rewards. We couldn't find reinforcements that would get them motivated. But once we told them they *couldn't* do something—a negative punishment because we took away something that they liked in order to decrease a targeted behavior—they responded really well. That's an effective punishment strategy.

Reinforcers

Primary reinforcers can be things that don't need to be conditioned or learned, such as food, drink, shelter, and warmth. *Secondary reinforcers* are those that are conditioned or learned or anything else that might increase the display of a certain behavior.

Reinforcers can be broken down into types, such as edible, sensory, tangible, activity and social, to name a few. Edible reinforcers are, of course, desirable foods. Sensory rewards bring pleasure of some kind, like hearing music, looking at art, or having a massage. Tangible reinforcers include toys, books, and video games that the kid enjoys. Activity reinforcers offer opportunities to have fun and might include activities such as playing mini golf or going for a walk. Socially rewarding reinforcers include visiting a friend or engaging in a preferred topic of conversation. Notice that some of these examples can overlap, and this might indicate greater potency for a particular child. Of course, any of these are only suitable as reinforcers if the child finds pleasure in them, whatever form they come in.

Here's an important point. When we work with a kid who is profoundly affected with an ASD or who has experienced trauma, social praise from an adult or teacher falls into the category of being a secondary reinforcer. In other words, this population may have to be taught, in a systematic way, what social praise is and what is meant by it. Many people think, "Oh, she's a child, so of course she is going to love me saying nice things to her!" But she actually might not receive it as gracefully and pleasurably as they might think. It can sometimes take time for children with ASD to learn why social praise should feel good. This is one of the reasons you see treatment centers starting with tangible reinforcers for many diagnosed kids. They have to go with the information they can gather about what the child takes pleasure in, especially if the kid doesn't yet have a good communication system in place.

Short, Fast, and Easily Accessible

Let's go back to Jason. If we know Jason likes M&M's and outdoor play, we might want to run with these most obvious reinforcers. Although they might work well in a few situations, we also need to come up with a list of reinforcements that are short, fast, and easily *delivered*—but not too easily *accessible*. In other words, it's not feasible to plan on rewarding the kid with a five-minute trip to the playground each time he is able to touch the correct letter out of a group of letters. Reinforcers need to be accessible to you, the person providing the treatment, and if they're too easily and frequently accessible to your child in other settings, he might not be motivated enough to do the task at hand.

This brings up the question of using edibles. Food can be a quick, easily accessible reward, for sure, but discrete trial training and other applied behavior analysis modalities sometimes get a bad rap for using food as reinforcers. But think about it. If that's the only thing that Tanisha's going to work for, and we're looking at extinguishing an unsafe behavior, it can be worth it. After all, there can often be a sense of urgency about it when destructive behaviors are involved. Studies show that aggression and self-injurious behaviors are the most stressful categories for caregivers. These types of behaviors, bring up the question of whether it's sometimes feasible to use food as a reinforcer in the early stages of treatment.

People ask me if it's right or okay to give kids junk food as a reinforcer. I've concluded that if you have a kid who's profoundly affected with the disorder—say, one who has layers of bruises because she is so self-injurious—would you be willing to give her half of a Gummy Bear every ten seconds if it means she doesn't hurt herself anymore? In my mind: *Absolutely.* As the behavior specialist, if I am going with Gummy Bears, then I have already ruled out other types of research-based protocols because they weren't effective. And of course, Gummy Bears aren't a long-term or permanent strategy, and we will reassess the program after a period of time.

You also have rules around edibles, too. When I was working in the schools, I made it very clear to the parents to never, ever give the kid the edibles we were using in class as a reward at home—except nutritious foods, of course. There were only rare exceptions to this rule.

Yes, it can get complicated. You do have to tease through the list and figure out which ones are the most practical and sustainable to work with. But it's worth it. Again, I need to emphasize that one size does *not* fit all as far as using edibles for reinforcement. I encourage you to work with a behavior specialist to assess all the benefits and risks before implementing any complex strategy.

The ideal short, fast, and easy reinforcement is praise, and we want to sprinkle in as many brief celebratory moments—praising the specific "job well done"—as much as possible. But, unlike other kids in the kindergarten class, many kids with ASD don't intuitively know that loud cheers and big smiles mean that they should *feel good*. Many of them evidence sensitivities, and such raucous cheering can sometimes actually have the effect of unintentionally startling and escalating them—the opposite effect we are aiming for. We do need to *teach* many kids that those kinds of expressions are intended to be supportive and reinforcing—and that knowledge will, in turn, help them slowly reduce dependency on prompts like edibles and other tangibles. Plus, praise is free and intangible, and by helping them learn its place, we help them build their socializing skills. In other words, they learn to associate the "party" with success, which in turn helps them learn to navigate the social world better.

People sometimes ask me, "Why do we have to give a kid something when they're just expected to do something? Isn't that a bribe?" Bribes usually happen when parents don't know how to use reinforcements effectively; for instance, when they find themselves caught up in a circumstance and they don't have a predetermined plan in place. In such conditions, they feel like they don't have any other leverage, so they often go with a bribe to get the result they want. After all, if you're at the checkout line at Walmart and your kid starts crying, you might be willing to do just about anything. "Look, I'll give you candy if you stop crying!" you might say. You're panicking, and you're the one emotionally at risk at the time. You don't want to feel worse or feel embarrassed and out of control. Then you're the one who is on the brink of losing in the transaction. When parents have more to lose with no pre-established plan in place, they generally opt for what would be considered a bribe. Sometimes it can't be helped. That's why it's so important to establish a strategy for reinforcements to be used even when your back is against the wall.

Elementary schools have a built-in structure in place for the day's activities, ensuring that the children's daily patterns are repeated and followed every day for the entire school year. That supports them in learning expectations and consistency. Not only are the kids learning expectations about behavior at school; they learn what the consequences of following and not following rules are. They see the same consequences for most of the kids with similar behaviors, and they learn how their behavior impacts others. This is highly beneficial for any child to learn to navigate society in general. Not surprisingly, kids need the same education at home. That's where reinforcement planning comes in.

Reinforcement Planning

To put it simply, reinforcements work best when delivered in a structured and consistent way. It is not wise to make them up at the moment; for example, when you're at a Walmart having a sudden reaction to a child's behavior. Effective reinforcements don't get created as a result of negotiations with the child in the moment, either. They're thoughtful, structured plans that the child is well informed about in advance and that you're able to stick to. I typically recommend to parents that after a plan is devised (with my assistance) that they talk to their kids about it in advance and do so in a deliberate setting—not while engaged in another activity at the same time. For example, if we aren't targeting a destructive type of behavior, we might roll out the plan on a Thursday and explain to the child that it will start the following Monday. That way, we have time to review the plan with the child several times, so he knows exactly what to expect.

You might find yourself frequently wondering, "Why can't my kid just _____?" *[fill in the blank]* If this happens, chances are you don't have a structured and consistent reinforcement plan in place to support your efforts. Just because the child was able and/or willing to perform a targeted behavior once doesn't mean he is able or willing do it every time he is asked. With a reinforcement plan, you make an agreement or contract with the child, and they either satisfy their agreement and get the reward, or they don't. The consistency helps you reduce their dependency on prompts and helps them build the skills you want them to learn, achieving independence. It's a structured, well-thought-out plan, and if you stick with it, you'll find that you won't need it forever.

Let's take a simple example. If little Jason, who has a formal diagnosis of ASD, needs to brush his teeth independently, his parents could first stop and take a look at the bigger picture. They'd begin to create a reinforcement inventory, a list consisting of the things that Jason loves more than anything. Jason is crazy about M&Ms, for example.

If the targeted behavior is for Jason to brush his teeth independently, his parents can start by looking at their inventory of possible reinforcements and rewards and weigh each one, trying to narrow the list to the best ones to use for the purpose. Which ones are the most appropriate, healthy, and accessible? If it's too accessible, will that undercut its effect as a reward? They'd also need to factor in whether it's a sustainable and realistic plan for them: Can they commit to the offered reward each time it is earned? Consistency and follow-through with the plan on the part of the parents are essential to success.

Finally, they would narrow the list down and choose the reinforcement of allowing Jason to go outside and play for 20 minutes, which he loves more than anything. Then, they'd communicate the plan to Jason, essentially creating an agreement or contract with him about what's going to happen.

"Okay, Jason, we're going to start to work on getting you to brush your teeth."

"Okay, Mom."

"So here's what's going to happen. Right after dinner, you're going to brush your teeth. And as soon as you finish brushing all your teeth, you can go outside for 20 minutes, no matter what."

"Really?"

"Yep! We'll come in the bathroom with you to get you started."

That's the start of the reinforcement part. Then come the prompts.

On the first day, when Jason goes to the bathroom to brush his teeth, he might say, "Help me, Mom! I need help!"

Mom responds, "You can do it. Here, I'll show you how to do it." And she puts the toothpaste on the brush for him. Then she wipes it off. He's got a clean toothbrush to start with.

"Okay. Now, you do it," she says.

If, to Mom's surprise, Jason successfully brushes his teeth, Mom learns that Jason actually had the skill all along; he just *wasn't willing* to brush his teeth. But now that she has a strong enough reward reinforcer working for her, the behavior is taken care of. If the assumption is that Jason has all of the skills to brush his teeth, then as soon as the boy follows through with a task completely—with no prompts—he gets to go outside for 20 minutes.

While this example is largely oversimplified, sometimes it can be this easy! Every situation will be different, of course, to reinforce the behavior you want and build the skills and independence that you want your children to build. You can start out with prompting and helping, too, but you have to have a plan in place to fade out that assistance, or you won't get the change you're hoping for.

Building a Foundation, Piece by Piece

Parents of kids who are not as profoundly affected by their ASD diagnosis don't always see the advantage of taking the applied behavior analysis-driven, "building-block" approach. They sometimes believe the strategies are causing their kid to backtrack and think their kid is being dumbed down. But the truth is, it's not easy to know what kids with ASD have really mastered and what they haven't. Some do get through an ABA program super quickly, and therapists are able to assess their skill set accurately. But sometimes behaviorists find they need to back up and evaluate whether or not there are any gaps in the child's executive functioning or demonstrations of skills. Even though a child might seem to be functioning quite well on the outside, it is quite common for them to have hidden latent executive functioning errors or gaps in their learning base. Those will have a significant effect on their behavior and will continue to interfere with their development as they grow up.

Splinter skills or *parcellated skills* are these basic or mid-level skills that are missing or not mastered even though some foundational skills and high-level skills related to them have been learned and demonstrated well. Kids with ASD can sometimes appear to be able to skip over mid-level steps while being able to accomplish a desired, higher-level skill. But even if they can perform the desired higher-level tasks, if the intermediary skills and concepts along the way are missing, it may slow down the child's ability to learn higher skills or even prevent the child from learning to perform other high-level skills that other kids in their age group are doing every day. This might become more evident as time goes on.

In fact, families who have avoided their child's diagnosis because they didn't want them to be burdened with the label often reach out to me when their child is in high school or college. As a result, many of the skills that they weren't sure were mastered often become glaringly evident, and there's a sudden urgent need for treatment to bolster and sustain daily functioning. The problem is that parents can no longer sustain the same degree of control over their young adult offspring through a reinforcement program as they could when the child was young. Additionally, a person diagnosed without tools can quickly escalate from frustration to physical aggression, which is a very unwanted consequence from an adult statured body.

Talk therapy alone can present many challenges. Because of executive function challenges, a sometimes very low frustration tolerance, lack of flexibility, and seeing the world as the problem for not fitting into their script, talk therapy can produce a very externalized view of blame in the mind of a person diagnosed with ASD. Additionally, statements like "I would feel better if that person hadn't done that to me," or "I would feel better if they get punished" are sometimes the insight. Resolution in the form of perceived justice becomes the only means of resolving feelings about a particular issue. Based on this reasoning, if it can't provide justice, therapy isn't always viewed as helpful or necessary, and the person might choose not to continue.

Applied Behavior Analysis can be designed to meet the developmental needs of youth of any age. I urge parents to do what is in everyone's best interest for the long run and seek treatment early.

To ensure that these kinds of errors and gaps are addressed, ABA's building-block approach simply works best. One young girl I worked with loved marshmallows, so we started her on simple tasks with marshmallows as her reinforcement choice. After every task or command, she got half of a mini marshmallow. Over time, if she accomplished something bigger, then she'd get a bigger reward after a few hours (delayed). She might get 15 or 30 minutes of playtime, for example, or a special activity, such as an art project, that she could do with a peer, which gave her an opportunity for social interaction as well. She'd also get social praise based on her accomplishments, all throughout the day. Over time, we transitioned her off of those minute-by-minute small task rewards (mini marshmallows) to much larger tasks and rewards, and at the same time, she was learning that social praise was giving her the feedback that she had done a good job. With that systematic, baby-step-like approach and the combination of rewards and learned praise, she eventually got to the point where she could successfully complete a whole day of school without the need for tangible or edible rewards along the way.

Concerns About ABA

As I've hinted, as ubiquitous and respected as ABA is, it does have its detractors. One of the criticisms that I've heard from therapists and clinicians about it is that they don't see it as acknowledging the emotional side of a person's life experience. "ABA is kind of rough," one teacher said to me. "I think it's hard on the kids. It doesn't take emotions into consideration." But that's not exactly true. One of the most common emotional disturbances I see in the ASD population is what is clinically diagnosed as "anxiety" and what parents sometimes call a "meltdown." I see it as emotional dysregulation that is lessened by the implementation of behavior modification and executive functioning applications. For this population, emotional dysregulation can be triggered by several things, including change, such as something unexpected happening or needs going unmet due to communication barriers. Can managing emotional dysregulation with these antecedents be taught, and can the child be taught to evidence better emotional regulation? Absolutely.

For the most part, people tend to address emotional regulation with a variety of overt behavioral techniques. ABA has the same goal, but it uses a more developmentally appropriate delivery system. If we follow the "clear, concise, and consistent" rules and guidelines of the

ABA methodology, we are teaching the child expectations. Doing so helps us help them develop transitioning skills—the ability to move from one thing to another in any type of environment and how to change directions.

For example, sometimes we work with children who don't have a sophisticated communication system, and the ABA approach helps us anticipate and hypothesize why they are experiencing a particular emotion—even if they can't tell us. We do that in the initial ABA assessment phases, carefully reviewing and assessing the situations in which the child appears to be more uncomfortable or in distress. That gives us information about what is behind the behaviors so we can more precisely respond to them. After all, many young people who are able to write and participate in online discussions talking about their experiences with ABA therapy may be a testament to the skills gained from the treatment.

Yes, with ABA, we focus on behaviors, but because of the methods and practices we use, the result is an upward shift in emotional content. Again and again, I find that behavioral improvements end up making everybody feel better. ABA does not ignore emotions or deep-seated emotional dysregulation work. However, emotional dysregulation in this population is often caused by not understanding and/or applying the correct formula or by the caregiver's perceived inflexibility. To the outside observer, the procedures might just look like a whole bunch of prompts and reinforcements, but they initiate meaningful change that makes everyone happier.

If we look deeper, we can understand why the ABA approach can look cold and mechanical from the outside. First, since all of our interactions are founded on communication, we know that the more we can get communication working smoothly, the more we can make progress. Language issues are inherently present in this population, so we wisely customize our language to suit them better. We start by paring down our sentences to the bare minimum. We speak in shorter sentences. We slow down our speech and break it down into simple words with intentional delivery. We also want to use a neutral volume and tone without a lot of inflection at first. And we do this consistently so kids begin to relax and feel that they can understand and be heard.

We have to be able to make sure that they understand and comprehend what we're saying. Once they have that language capacity, we build on it under the direction of speech pathologists.

But parents sometimes get triggered by how it looks. When professionals use ABA methods to teach kids with ASD, it's usually in a highly structured environment. They're often sitting in a chair, close to their desk or at a table with their feet on the ground and the best readiness posture. Then they're doing repetitive tasks or drills. They're being asked, "What letter (is this)?" or "What number (is this)?" It looks pretty mechanical.

On the other hand, parents are used to seeing the typical kindergarten classroom where the teacher keeps up a fast pace of stimulating banter with a slightly elevated voice. They do this to keep the attention of the kids at that age. "How's everybody feeling today? OK! Let's do this!" they might say. They'll spill out a lot of words even as they express nonverbal, social communication like smiling, exaggerated facial expressions, and opening their eyes wide. Parents usually love this. They consider it "warm and fuzzy" and think, "That's what my kid needs—love and comfort!"

But when they see their child sitting quietly at a table, working with an ABA therapist, receiving seemingly dry, elemental instructions, it looks quite different, and they get concerned. They wonder why their kid isn't getting those same warm and fuzzies the teacher gives in the classroom.

But the simple truth is that the paths of social and communication development for the two groups are significantly different. Remember, ASD is a developmental disorder. The ASD population generally responds poorly to being overstimulated. It takes them longer to parse verbal and nonverbal cues, and most don't really have the gestural translation skills to understand, first, that these are rewards and, second, what they need to do to receive them, for example. These characteristics are generally inherent in the diagnosis. While many kids who've never been diagnosed with ASD can keep up with the teacher, kids with ASD might become dysregulated to such an extent that they're unable to pay attention at all.

Yes, ABA can appear sterile to an observer, but research proves that its design is a well-suited and appropriate teaching tool for this disorder. And DTT, which emphasizes a quiet environment and a limited number of pared-down instructions expressed in a clear, concise, and consistent way, is specifically designed for this population.

The Path of Skill Development with Applied Behavior Analysis

When I worked at Family Behavior Resources, one of my great inspirations was Ralph Wilps, Jr., PhD, a clinical psychologist and a consultant to managed care companies in Pennsylvania. Much of his work centered on helping caregivers understand problematic behaviors in those diagnosed with ASD, and his understanding of ASD behavior has had a profound effect on me and my work.

He described three phases of skill development in the ASD-diagnosed group that help give us a sense of how we might expect progression to go when ABA is done correctly. Over the years, I've found this perspective very useful to help me explain to the many parents I have worked with how their child's skill development might unfold as we successfully extinguished unwanted behaviors and added desirable behaviors that are more socially acceptable. He uses interesting, evocative names for the phases to help give us a better appreciation for each one. Be mindful that this is his guideline and each child's developmental level will vary.

Wilps called the first phase the "addict phase." Wilps generally explained it as being especially evident in children with limited vocalizations or functional communication who are profoundly affected with the disorder. An example of a child in this phase with respect to communication might be undergoing an assessment for an appropriate communication method, or they might be in the early stages of learning a communication method through sign language or the help of a device. This child has very basic to low communicative skills at this point. When kids are in the addict phase, they tend to get gratification through self-stimulatory or self-injurious behaviors—something sensory-based. Wilps said he chose the word "addict" because the pain that these kids sometimes inflict on themselves can raise their endorphin levels and give sensory feedback in the form of a high, so to speak. Essentially, it's a repetitive neural feedback loop. Self-injurious behaviors are some of the most challenging behaviors to extinguish, but they're not impossible to dissolve.

The second phase, called the "recovering stroke victim phase," happens when caretakers or professionals are able to eliminate some of the presenting problematic, aggressive, or self-injurious behaviors. Wilps chose the name for the phase because it reminds us of a person who has just suffered a stroke and has lost some skills. They might be aware of their environment and know what they need to do, but they won't be able to accomplish the necessary skills to navigate their environment or complete tasks. Similarly, for the ASD-diagnosed population, it's as if they have the information stored within them somehow, but they have a challenge putting it together to be able to express themselves appropriately and accurately. For this population, "putting it together" becomes a process; it doesn't necessarily come naturally as it does for many others. For this reason, they will need guidance to help them assimilate information and express it.

Wilps dubs the third phase "a foreigner in a foreign land." If you're walking the streets of a foreign country, you might not be confident about using the language, you might not be able to communicate very well, but you can blend in. Sometimes you might make a social gesture that matches what a native of that country might offer you, whether it's appropriate or not. Those who are in this phase of development need refinement of their social communication skills in different settings, which will likely include being able to read nonverbal cues correctly and being able to problem-solve at higher levels while assessing social interactions.

Forty or fifty years ago, even after the DSM came out with its new definitions of autism spectrum disorder, few, if any, adults were diagnosed and identified with it; the public was only getting insights about ASD from a handful of courageous people, such as Temple Grandin. Google hadn't been invented yet; you couldn't just go online and look something up, either. Wilps' stages helped me explain how the typical progression of skills within the ABA model might look to the many hopeless parents who were short on information and didn't know what to expect. As simple as these phases can appear, caregivers have been able to rely on them and gain a greater understanding of what their children might be experiencing.

* * * * *

In the first phases of working with a child using ABA methodology, we review and assess the situations in which the child's behavior goes awry. In the next chapter, we'll look more closely at Functional Behavioral Assessment, a system that helps us get a lot more information about the why's and when's of those behaviors along with their antecedents and consequences. These insights enable us to develop much more targeted and more effective strategies for minimizing troublesome behaviors and nourishing desired ones.

4

Assessment Tools

B ehaviors, for anyone, can be tricky to observe and understand, but that's especially true when it comes to the ASD-diagnosed population. It's common and easy to draw quick conclusions about someone's behavior based on our personal experience and any conclusions we've drawn about behaviors long before we really get complete and accurate data about it. So, to help those with ASD dismantle maladaptive behaviors and learn new constructive ones, we have to look more deeply than our preconceptions so we can understand their behaviors with more discernment and precision. We also have to take the time to learn what is motivating and inciting problematic behaviors, what is impeding desired ones. We have to let go of many assumptions and sentiments and do some digging to be able to draw a more accurate picture of what is really going on. That will be essential when it comes time to start picking reinforcement and punishment strategies to help improve behaviors. We will be more informed about the real issues, we will waste less time, and our efforts will be significantly more productive in a shorter amount of time.

Functional Behavioral Assessment

Functional Behavioral Assessment (FBA) is a behavior analysis process used within ABA for identifying problem behaviors and developing interventions to improve or eliminate those behaviors. It focuses on helping behavioral health care professionals uncover what's behind the activation of certain behaviors in order to guide the development and selection of appropriate treatment. Whether or not you decide to have your child undergo the formal FBA process with a professional, it's incredibly helpful to look at behaviors through the FBA lens.

An FBA consists of information-gathering procedures that help behaviorists hypothesize about why a behavior is occurring. The process helps identify the environmental antecedents and consequences that help sustain the behavior, and the gathered information is used to develop an effective and efficient behavior plan. Best practices dictate that parental consent is obtained before an FBA is conducted with a minor.

In behavioral language, the FBA process helps us uncover the "function" of a behavior—in other words, the "why" behind it. What purpose does the behavior serve? Why is the youth engaging in that type of behavior? What are they trying to get by doing the behavior, or what are they trying to avoid? Answers to these questions help us understand the motivating factors behind behaviors. Ultimately, this precision of information allows us to target the problematic behavior more accurately—in all its complexity—and begin to see improvements much more quickly.

The complex nature of behaviors speaks to the need for intervention by behavioral therapists to investigate and begin to understand what is motivating the child and what are some of the underlying triggers to their maladaptive behaviors. In therapy, the behaviorist acts like a detective, asking questions, getting a more detailed and accurate picture of what happened when things went wrong.

For example, if the child reports, "That kid said that to me," the behaviorist would invite them to go back and remember the situation in order to try to paint the picture in greater detail. "Let's go back to when that happened," they'd say and then they'd ask helpful questions. "Where were you? What was going on with other people? Did they have a smile on their face? Were they giggling?" And so on. Or if the kid was at a dance and out of nowhere gets upset, the adults in the room might say: "I don't know what happened! everything was fine! And then he just freaked out!" They wouldn't be able to discern what the antecedent was. But a behaviorist would have him recount the experience, ask the kid what happened, and find out that he had dropped his drink all over the place, and that kind of thing had never happened to him before. It was a new situation that the child might not have known how to react to or handle. Kids diagnosed with ASD are generally not likely to volunteer the subtle aspects of the situation. That is why asking these questions is often necessary, and even though we know that memories can be distorted, asking these questions can still provide much context.

It's very doable to get to the bottom of things if you ask the right questions, and behaviorists ask strategic questions in order to uncover what the antecedents and triggers of an upset are. What they learn provides keys to what issues to address and treat and help them make priorities about what issues have the most impact and so should be worked with first.

Without systematic tools to formally assess behaviors, it's human nature to generalize about behaviors and think we have identified them accurately. For example, it might seem acceptable to say that a child had a "tantrum" the other day. But when we are working with kids with ASD and want to communicate their behavior to another caregiver or professional, the word doesn't tell us much. The truth is, one kid's tantrum can look strikingly different from the next kid's tantrum! One kid might be lying on the floor pounding his fist, and the other might be sitting in a chair screaming in protest. In both of these cases, "tantrum" won't be a precise enough definition for parents and professionals to communicate to each other about what the child actually did, and it won't be sufficient to help either of them devise a potent and meaning-ful plan for to help improve behaviors in the future.

This principle was demonstrated to me in a high school English class I took years ago—long before I knew anything about ABA. The teacher brought two students up to the front of the class and then read to them a passage from some classic literature. As he read, the students had to act out what he was describing, and sure enough, they each ended up enacting two very different scenes. Likewise, when we begin defining behaviors, we have to get out of our heads and emotions and identify exactly what's happening.

Suppose someone has received instructions about what to do when the child has a tantrum. If the child starts to pound their fists on a table, should they consider that a tantrum? Is that what the observer meant by "tantrum"? Or should they wait until the feet start stomping as well to consider it a tantrum? If we use too vague of a word, like "tantrum," there will be too much room for others to misinterpret and misunderstand. It will also set up the rest of the FBA process for major pitfalls. It becomes far easier to administer treatment strategies when we use and communicate highly specific descriptions of behaviors.

Many other often-misused terms besides "tantrum" are tossed around a lot as parents and professionals alike attempt to describe the behaviors of kids with spectrum disorders. I've heard people describe a child as being "off-task," for example, but what does that tell us about what he was doing? Do we have any insight into what was happening beforehand or what other behaviors they were exhibiting? If a first grader with sloppy handwriting gets up and wanders around the room, someone might want to label them as having "attention issues." But if we don't ask questions, we will probably miss important pieces of the puzzle. Did anyone ask the kid, for example, if they're having trouble writing letters—or seeing clearly? Other terms thrown around that don't convey much specificity include "bad attitude," "lazy," "low self-esteem," "frustrated," "just wants control," "just wants power," "just trying to push my buttons," "angry," "lack of motivation," and "disrespectful."

The reason that these are not clear examples of behavior is that the terms are so general they communicate very little. They're very hard to quantify or replicate. As we enter into behavioral assessment, we need to be able to define a behavior so clearly that any person can reproduce it based on the description provided. I've noticed that whenever treatment plans aren't effective, one of the main reasons is that the targeted behavior is defined way too broadly. This initial definition drives the rest of the process.

It's also incredibly important—especially if we're parents—to take on an objective perspective of the child's behavior. It's a big ask, but we have to remember to set our emotions aside and not interpret behaviors as reactions to us personally. We need to look at behaviors through a neutral and objective lens. We can't simply listen to our feelings to tell us why the child is behaving the way they are. They're not doing anything just "to get back at" us, for example—a sentiment I often hear from parents. When we look at things with a clear eye, we become more effective at intervening with the problematic behavior. We also won't get burned out so quickly. The FBA process happens to be quite powerful to help train our brains to look at behaviors objectively.

Discovering the Why's

One of the first steps in the FBA process is to gather information. After we have gathered information and clearly defined our targeted behavior, we need to determine the function or functions of the particular behavior we want to change.

There are many different types of actual tools one can use at various stages of the FBA process. When considering how to determine the function of a behavior and the unique motivations behind it, one of the most effective tools is the Motivational Assessment Scale, or MAS. The original version, developed by Durand and Crimmins in 1988, has been revised, providing more detail, and is referred to as the MAS-II. I refer to the original version here for simplicity's sake, which is easier to dive into.

Used primarily by behaviorists, the MAS is a rating scale designed to help identify what's motivating a problematic behavior. The original MAS guides professionals to first define a behavior and then answer specific questions about that behavior. It is a 51-item questionnaire that asks the respondent to rate each item on a scale of 1 to 6 and takes about 15 to 30 minutes to complete. Here are a few sample questions to give you an idea of them:

» Would the behavior occur continuously, over and over, if the person was left alone for long periods of time?

» Does the behavior occur when others are attending to him or her?

» Would the behavior repeatedly occur, in the same way, for very long periods of time if no one was around?

» Does the behavior occur when a request is made of the person?

Maybe you're now getting an idea of why we need to be so specific when we work to define a behavior!

When done by professionals, the Motivational Assessment Scale can help us understand the problem behavior, its antecedents, and its related consequences, and those can help us generate hypotheses about the motivations of the behavior or *why* it is happening. The inquiry needs to be done carefully, patiently, and professionally; it might take a bit of time to get all the information possible to form a clear enough picture of the behavior to begin formulating intervention strategies. Finally, the MAS should be completed by all adults who have frequent contact with the child.

The original Motivational Assessment Scale offers four categories of functions that might apply to any behavior:

1. Sensory—to experience sensory feedback or stimulation or to meet a sensory need

2. Tangible—to get access to something tangible or to get something in hand

3. Escape Demands—to escape from or avoid people, tasks, or activities

4. Attention-seeking—to gain attention of any kind

The updated MAS—the MAS-II—expanded the inquiry further to 57 questions and split the Escape Demands function into two: Escape Demands and Escape Attention, resulting in a total of five potential functions of behaviors.

When I am doing this with parents and professionals for the first time, I typically choose not to list and explain these functions before the process so that no biases are created. If I pre-suppose that a certain behavior is attention-seeking, that bias might reflect in how I answer each item, looking to make sure that is the end-game function. But that is not objective.

Everybody has some sensory-seeking behavior, such as chewing gum, smoking, and tapping a finger. It's just a matter of degree and safety that determines whether it is problematic. It's generally thought that people engage in sensory seeking to obtain feedback for their own gratification around the senses, and even potentially their thoughts. They're engaging in a behavior that makes them feel good. Individuals can demonstrate variability in what behaviors are sensory seeking. Again, the degree to which these types of behaviors interfere with daily life and well-being determines when they are problematic.

Sensory-seeking behaviors among the ASD-diagnosed can revolve around any of the senses, but visual ones are often the easiest to observe. Sometimes we see kids, especially younger kids, with this diagnosis looking at lights, staring, cocking their head looking a certain way, or getting very close to something to look at it. *Other sensory-seeking behaviors are tactile in nature, for example, touching certain textures or certain objects* repeatedly, more intensely, or more frequently. One can also exhibit an overfocus on auditory behaviors, such as having to listen to something. I've worked with kids who would get very close to their laptops or other devices and want to hear some sound—over and over again, continuously hitting replay or rewind. Sensory-seeking vocal behaviors might consist of different types of repetitive vocalizations or even nonsensical sounds that are repeated over and over again. These are usually highly evident—even to the untrained. Sensory-seeking behaviors involving smell and taste can include sniffing, tasting, or licking objects inappropriately.

The other three functions are a bit more straightforward to explain. A tangible function would be to get something one can touch or have in hand, such as a toy, money, or food. Attention function is just that. If we put aside our presumptions that trying to get attention is "bad," seeking attention can come across as maladaptive, although the child might be genuinely trying to tell someone something. Remember, inherent in this diagnosis are communication issues. Escape means just trying to avoid something. For example, if the child with messy handwriting left his seat, we could hypothesize that the writing work is too difficult, and the child is trying to avoid it.

Not surprisingly, we often find that there is more than one function for a specific behavior; much of the time, with this population, the function is not going to fall neatly into just one category. If a child is hitting, for example, it might be serving both a sensory-seeking function as well as an attention-seeking function. On the other hand, these functions might not apply to other children's hitting behaviors. I find that problematic behaviors that parents have difficulty working through themselves are usually serving multiple functions.

We also want to identify under what specific conditions we observe the behavior. For example, the child might only have been observed hitting another person in the lunchroom. Another child might only attempt to run out of the classroom at a certain time of day. These conditions give us more specific information to better build a strategy to address the targeted behavior.

Administering the Functional Behavioral Assessment

The FBA methodology is typically included in the Individualized Education Plan (IEP), a document used by public school staff and behavioral professionals that identifies the support that a child with an identifiable disability will need to make academic and behavioral progress. In a public-school setting, the people involved in IEP planning and supervision might include the child's teachers, the behavior specialist, and the school psychologist. Then, in collaboration with the parent, the team begins to implement ABA methodology by building antecedent and consequence strategies that fit the functions at play. After the initial assessment process, the team would continue to observe and collect data on a child's overt behavior in order to assess if the plan adequately addresses the proposed functions of the behaviors on an ongoing basis. If the undesired behavior is decreasing, and the desired behavior is increasing, then the plan is working.

To be clear, FBA isn't only used with youth diagnosed with ASD. In most school systems, students who exhibit significant behavioral problems that interfere with schoolwork daily will undergo the FBA process as well.

To begin, the child's behaviors are prioritized so that destructive behaviors are dealt with first, disruptive behavior second, and disturbing behaviors the last to be addressed. It can take weeks for those involved in the FBA process to gather the necessary information from the numerous people who are involved in the child's life. If the behavior specialists find that some of the respondents answer the questions differently from others, they have to try to make sense of it all, by asking more questions later and then making decisions about how to reconcile and respond to the differences. There might be discussions about whether they have targeted the optimal behavior for the inquiry. Or maybe a teacher or a parent didn't observe something that others did. People often think about the questions in different way, too. It's a complicated process, and every child is, of course, unique, so assumptions can't be made. There's no checklist that can be checked off item by item. Many informed judgment calls have to be made.

In order to meet its training needs, the state of Pennsylvania devised a statewide training program for those providing in-home services to better serve the ASD population. Once I obtained my behavior specialist license in 2012, I had the opportunity to train behavior specialists to conduct FBAs. At the time, the Pennsylvania State Bureau of Autism Services' FBA Training provided the following seven recommended steps for administering an FBA. Although it has been updated since then, this part of the process has remained relatively unchanged.

Evaluating and figuring out the function of a behavior is ultimately a fairly intricate process. Plus, I find that the skill to perform FBAs is largely gained through experience. No two children are the same, so there are never going to be cookie-cutter interpretations of behaviors or strategies to improve any one specific behavior. Board certified behavior analysts (BCBAs) and behavior specialists become much more informed about what questions they can ask as follow-up and where to drill down when there are enigmas through their experience over time.

7- Step Functional Behavioral Assessment Process

Step 1: Prioritize and define the behavior.

Step 2: Collect data indirectly. Interview people around the child to get their opinions on the behavior. Review any records, evaluations, and data about the child.

Step 3: Collect data directly through direct observation. This involves watching the child or student and taking detailed, quantitative notes regarding a specific behavior.

Step 4: Analyze the data.

Step 5: Develop and test the proposed hypothesis about the conditions under which the specific behavior in question occurs

Step 6: Design and devise a support plan or treatment plan, including strategies and interventions.

Step 7: Monitor and evaluate the plan.

I also like to caution that the people administering and participating in the FBA process need to have a lot of objectivity to help the team come up with as precise and helpful conclusions as they can. If someone loves the kids so much that they just want them to be loved and get hugged, it's just not enough. That kind of sensibility ends up overriding the rational mind when engaging in an FBA process. The person needs to want to help the child get better, above all else, and be willing to set preconceptions and emotional attachments aside to do that.

Then there's the question of resiliency, which I will discuss in much more depth in later chapters when I discuss how caregivers can avoid exhaustion and learn to manage their energy for their own sake as well as the child's. A person can be good at doing what they do, but if they aren't able to be resilient, they're going to crash eventually. To support resiliency, those involved in administering FBAs need to have what I call "neutral passion"—a mindset that allows you to work passionately, but still you're not so attached to the outcome that you burn out. After all, the outcomes of an FBA aren't always spot on the first time, and we might have to keep going back to the drawing board again and again to reassess and review. Emotional passion won't see people through that. However, a detached determination to find out what is best for the child will.

In most areas of the United States, most facilities prefer that those conducting FBAs are either Board-Certified Behavior Analysts (BCBAs) or clinically licensed in another capacity. But keep in mind that there is no comprehensive set of rules for conducting an FBA, only guidelines to follow. So, one can be good at the science, for example, but there is no substitute for the insights gleaned through experience. Additionally, the BCBA training programs do not include psychotherapy components, although some ethics are covered. Psychotherapeutic techniques are reserved for licensed professionals in clinical fields such as psychology, counseling, and social work, which, I believe, can be the cause of some licensed professionals giving the profession a bad rap. Some complain that the FBA is not addressing emotions specifically enough, as I discussed earlier. But, appropriately, that is just not the behavior specialist's first line of strategy. Theirs is a different path to results.

Behaviors are so much more involved and complex than they seem on the surface. In fact, they are very often intricate, varied, and convoluted. So, yes, when working to understand the what's, how's, and why's of a maladaptive behavior, it will probably require time and patience to uncover the pieces of the puzzle underlying the issue and develop strategies to propel improvements. It can be very easy to fall into the trap of seeing and describing behaviors in somewhat vague and sweeping terms, but it ultimately doesn't serve you or your child to do so. It's also helpful to learn that problematic behaviors are serving at least one underlying "function"—they are in some way fulfilling some unseen need of the child. These insights help us have more compassion for those diagnosed as ASD as well as help us more accurately pinpoint the underlying issues that set the behaviors in play. Looking at behaviors through the FBA lens helps us bring about real change in the child's behaviors.

♦ ♦ ♦ ♦ ♦

Now that this and the previous chapters have equipped you with a deeper appreciation and understanding of the inner workings of ASD as well as an inside look at the industry's most respected methods for assessment and treatment, it's time to turn your attention to *you*, dear caregiver. What's it like from your perspective to manage the shockingly overwhelming task of managing the life and development of a person with ASD? Let's take an honest look at that so you get a clear and fairly comprehensive idea of how, where and why all your energy is getting drained in the process. Only then can we begin to talk about how to reclaim your energy, shore up your reserves, learn methods to stay balanced and, yes, sane, so that you can re-energize your life.

5

The Stresses and Strains of Parental Caregiving

Being the caregiver of a child with ASD brings a new reality for parents. From the first diagnosis to the countless appointments with physicians, therapists, and school personnel, parents of children with ASD—and by "parents," I refer to biological parents, adopted parents, or guardians—wake up one morning realizing that their world has changed dramatically. They have to re-evaluate their hopes, dreams, and expectations for their child and realize their child's future will be far different than they had planned for them. Their own lives are changed significantly, too. They find themselves confronted with behaviors that are confusing, unexpected, frustrating, and cause for alarm, and they begin to recognize that they will need to focus much more attention on the child and their development than they ever expected to. Of course, parenting a child can be challenging for anyone, but parenting a child with ASD can demand significantly more time, sacrifice, focus, problem-solving, learning, and work. And it's not a short-term problem to solve. It will most assuredly continue throughout the child's years in school and likely beyond.

In this chapter, I am candid with you about those realities. I talk about many of the stressors and challenges of life as a parent of a child with ASD. If this world is new to you, the chapter will inform you about many things you can expect to have to deal with. If you have been a parent of a diagnosed child for a while, this will serve to validate your experiences. Yes, it's a lot, but being honest with ourselves about the battle we are trying to win will only empower us. In the meantime, it's a no-holds-barred discussion, so buckle up.

Let's start by talking about the behaviors that a diagnosed child can exhibit—those behaviors that can be emotionally challenging for the caregiver to witness and somehow deal with. Starting with the basics—sleeping, eating, and toilet training—it is often quite difficult to get a child who is diagnosed on some kind of sleep schedule that we might consider "regular." Sure, non-diagnosed kids can have trouble sleeping, too, but kids who are diagnosed can sometimes take months or even years beyond the time it takes a typically developing child to get a sleep schedule locked in. And even then, they still might have a unique sleep pattern. On the other hand, some diagnosed kids can have very rigid sleep patterns that are very annoying to those around them.

Other behaviors they might exhibit include poor handwriting and difficulty with tasks such as lacing, zipping, and buttoning, and/or they might have a hard time using eating utensils, too, as their grip strength and fine motor skills can be poor. Or they might exhibit gross motor skill delays resulting in what appears to be clumsiness or uncoordinated-looking behaviors. They might have poor toileting behaviors, too; some can exhibit on-cue vomiting skills, which can be horrifying for parents to witness, especially in front of others.

Kids who are diagnosed can interact with objects somewhat strangely and inappropriately. They might try to put inedible objects in their mouths, or they might want to carry objects around all day long and frequently try to lick them or eat them. They might be over-focused on one object or do unusual things like play with their saliva and extend it up to the light.

Impulse control—with or without observable antecedents—is frequently observed by kids with ASD, and that can create a lot of havoc and upset. The child might say the "wrong" thing—often something socially unacceptable—to the wrong person at the wrong time. One child saying to another child, "You're fat," might trigger just about everybody in the vicinity. This can get especially problematic by the time the child gets to middle school, where social constructs dictate that the child should "know better" by then.

Diagnosed kids often have a hard time sitting still or staying in one place. They might run around or need a frequent change of environment. Or else they need to keep replaying known quantities, whether it's driving the same route to a destination or having an excessive loyalty to a specific brand and product of food. It can be exhausting when little Jason refuses to eat any other form of chicken besides Stouffer's chicken nuggets.

Or the child might say the same thing over and over again. As we've seen, those diagnosed usually operate by way of formulas, although it may not be readily apparent to us. Alternatively, they might fill in the time with memorized content, such as a few preferred sentences from a book or movie.

Some diagnosed kids can be physically stand-offish and don't want to be touched. They can seem to be inconsolable, which can be frustrating and confusing to parents, or they can be the opposite, wanting to be touching others often. These are examples of *sensory dysregulation*, which can also extend to those exhausting episodes that take hours and hours just to get the child to take a shower, get their hair cut, or brush their teeth. For example, one child might take five hours to get their nails cut and might only tolerate it once a month regardless of how much the parent complains about not liking to see their child going around looking ungroomed.

Kids with ASD also typically lack *incidental social learning*—the ability to learn from and pick up cues from others in their environment. Tone of voice, facial expressions, and even the volume of the voice communicate a lot to most of us. Children who aren't diagnosed typically begin picking up on those cues throughout their development, seemingly by osmosis, or intuitively. It's a whole layer of language they are able to absorb. Plus, they get some internal gratification and reinforcement when they modify their behavior to match environmental cues such as Mom's smiles or hugs.

But these same cues can consistently go unnoticed by kids with ASD. The nonverbal signals between schoolmates, the disapproving facial expression of a teacher, and the hurt tone in a sibling's voice simply won't be processed. Another way to say it is that the overlooked cues don't have meaning for them with respect to the formulas they've learned and stored for themselves.

I worked with a young man in middle school who told me that some girls in his class would pass him in the hallway and say, "Hi, R." What he didn't detect was that they said it to him with a taunt in their tone of voice and soft giggles afterward. In the meantime, R thought the girls liked him and were just saying hi. He missed a whole layer of information that was being communicated. Kids diagnosed simply require a long-term, focused, and structured course of learning to learn this new language of social cues. Truthfully, it is nearly impossible to teach what to expect and interpret in *every* situation.

Savant or Not?

One of the most common stereotypes you'll find applied to a diagnosed kid—which are often hammered home in the media—is that they are a savant or genius. Here's one kid that's especially brilliant in math; here's another that has memorized all the capital cities of the world by the time she was three. But what isn't publicized along with these spectacular feats is that those children are often actually missing other skills that usually develop at an early age. They might not be able to tie their shoes, hold a pencil long enough to write a word, or type on a keyboard functionally. And when they enter school and are in a position to learn alongside their fellow schoolmates, they are missing some of the basic skills and concepts that are often the foundation for more advanced and complex learning as they get older. So even though they might be able to do some things extremely well, things might look good on the surface,, but beneath the surface, there are chunks of information that haven't been wired in yet to enable them to function and problem-solve for themselves. Additionally, repeatedly doing some of skills that they're strong at doesn't necessarily help the other areas of cognition develop.

When these kids run into experiences that require skills they don't have, they might call on what they do know. For example, if you put a 15-year-old diagnosed kid in a social situation, they might run their script for chit-chat, and they appear to have mastered the social interaction. They know how to interact with "How are you?" and "I'm good." But if something unexpected or novel occurs that they don't have a formula for, they won't know how to respond, and they can react in unusual or escalated ways or say nothing at all. And, yes, this can also be stressful for them.

Adding to the parents' frustration is that, in the eyes of the professional supervising the situation, "everything seemed to be going along just fine." Most teachers and others in supervisory positions aren't trained to recognize early signs of escalation or identify when an executive functioning error occurs, and they might just shrug their shoulders, perplexed. Most don't have the resources to buffer an outburst or how to clean up any damage afterward, either. This is usually when people make the mistake of using sensory feedback to help the child calm down and feel better. They might offer them something soothing, such as a preferred object, to calm them down. On the surface, one might think, "Well, what's wrong with that if it helps him calm down?" If we go back to functions of behavior, this preferred object serves to reinforce an actual maladaptive behavior, and as the child has engaged with the object, they might have escaped engaging with something else that they didn't prefer. But the feedback can foster other layers of maladaptive behaviors. After all, teachers often have 25 or so other students to attend to, and they can't be expected to notice if a child isn't picking up social cues and responding to them in expected ways. The parents will have to find ways to avoid and rectify those situations. This is why a skilled behaviorist might be appropriate and highly beneficial for some kids in the school setting.

Further, by the age of four or five, children are typically able to recognize that other people have their own thoughts and feelings different from theirs—an important cognitive skill known as *theory of mind*—but many kids with ASD are slow to develop it or find it to be a lifelong challenge. With this skill underdeveloped, the child might not be able to consider that their playmate has their own needs or wants, and that can be off-putting to their potential friends and peers, as the diagnosed child might appear selfish and unengaged. Incidental learning might be lacking if the child isn't able to develop friendships or if they lack healthy physical boundaries.

Safety Issues

As mentioned in an earlier chapter, diagnosed kids will have what may appear to the rest of us as "glitches" in their executive functioning skills, one of the common ones being inhibition. Inhibition is our ability to stop and think before we do something; it is one thing that helps keep us safe as we look before we leap. But those with an error in the area of inhibition *don't* stop and think—they just get carried away with whatever impulse occurs to them. The impulse overtakes all other thinking, or the skill of hesitating to think it through that the other kids demonstrate doesn't come into play. As a result, our ASD-diagnosed kids are much more susceptible to safety mishaps than the average child. If they see something across the street that captures their interest, they might just run across the street without checking if there's any traffic coming first. They might touch a hot stove or try to step out of a moving car. Or they might unlock their seatbelt in the car and try to crawl up on the parent, or worse, pull their hair or put their hands in front of their face while the parent is trying to drive. Lack of self-awareness combined with a lack of impulse control can lead to scary situations. The seemingly paradoxical thing about safety situations is that, when they're not in the given situation, the child can probably tell you what they should or shouldn't do. This is part of why impulse control and inhibition is frustrating for parents and caregivers to experience. It's also very possible that other foundational, executive functioning skills might also need to be developed.

Sibling Issues Emerge

Adding another level to the mounting pile of things for a parent of an ASD-diagnosed child to manage is when that child has one or more older siblings. Parents are forced into a position of deciding how they're going to continue to manage the older child and meeting the demands of their academic and social life on top of all that they're doing for their diagnosed child.

The birth order of the child can also affect how much the diagnosis affects the peace and equanimity of the family, although it varies for every family. If the diagnosed child is the firstborn, it can sometimes be a devastating blow to the parents' hopes for their children. In any case, a non-diagnosed child in the family will take a back seat to the time-intensive planning and therapies of the diagnosed child at some point. If less attention is given, maladaptive behaviors in the other children can emerge, too. Or, responsibility might be thrust onto an older sibling, putting them into a quasi-caregiver role. A sibling might also struggle with feelings of grief and loss due to having a sibling that doesn't develop linearly in the way they might expect. Sadly, siblings can also be realistically afraid of their diagnosed sibling because of their aggressive and unpredictable behaviors. If the diagnosed child wasn't the firstborn, older siblings sometimes suffer from feeling that the amount of attention they once received has drastically diminished over time.

First Days at School

As the child enters the classroom for the first time, they might have difficulty adjusting to some aspects of their new surroundings, things that parents might have adjusted *for* them at home. Likewise, bringing their child to school for the first time can be intimidating for parents, too. They wonder how teachers will tease out their child's learning priorities and then navigate them. The demands of the new set of experiences seem to hit them all at once, especially those who harbor the hope that the difficulties might melt away once school starts—or that the school staff would know exactly what to do to further their child's education and assimilation into the school environment. Those few parents that are prepared know it's going to be a demanding journey ahead.

Taking a child to their first day of school is almost always a heart-wrenching event; almost every parent has to go through some emotional adjustment as they hand their kids over to other people's care and supervision. But when the child is diagnosed with ASD, that compounds the concerns and makes the experience even more stressful. The child might not have developed communication skills; they might not be expressing their needs or thoughts well at all yet. Similarly, and more upsetting for parents, is the concern that they might not be able to report events. For a while now, the parent has learned to work with the child, even anticipate their needs, taking care of them that way. Now, the parent is faced with handing the child over to someone with no such experience or intimacy with the child—and their mind fills with questions. Will they be able to survive the new environment? What about all the "what ifs"? They wonder how they can deal with the person that doesn't know their child anywhere close to the way they know them. Teacher meet-and-greets can help, but they certainly don't eliminate all the concerns for parents.

Furthermore, teachers often want to keep parents informed about the progress and performance of their child, especially parents of kids with behavioral or learning challenges. Parents are sometimes surprised to find themselves on the receiving end of a phone call every day, hearing about the child's upsets, and feeling helpless. Parents who have informed themselves about the potential unpleasant behaviors of kids diagnosed with ASD might spend the day petrified about what might happen in school and are constantly on edge. Plus, there's always the looming potential of a call to schedule a meeting to discuss alternative educational placements, which can be devastating for inexperienced parents. And calls of all sorts become the new normal more days than not—it's a "good day" if no call or email comes. Enmeshed in all of this, the parent starts to experience another layer of anxiety relating to sending the child to school. And the roller coaster ride can be incredibly exhausting.

Next, parents have to watch how their child fares socially. One of the most heart-wrenching sights is that of a child being shunned or bullied by other kids. Maybe in the child's early years, the parents had been able to find playdates or figure out which kids were tolerant of their child's unusual behaviors. But when it's time for the child to go to school, parents learn pretty quickly that most other kids don't adjust to them very well.

Young kids on the autism spectrum often have their own rules and well-defined scripts for playing that are unique to them, and they might insist that those they play with will follow along—which can drive peers away. For the parents, it can be very painful to think that their child doesn't have friends to play with. But, to be fair, some of the parents' bad feelings come from their projecting their own emotions onto their child. They might assume that the child feels lonely; after all, the parent would feel lonely if they were in that situation. But some diagnosed kids are actually content playing on their own. Others do attempt to interact, indicating a desire; they just might not have the skills they need to be successful at making friends.

In fact, therapists often recommend that diagnosed kids be exposed to age-appropriate peers in order to help them learn social skills. Since families need to make the effort to find playdates or groups for their child to participate in, this is stressful. They need to ask themselves tough questions about the level of aggression and safety of their kid. Plus, once a good play date is found, the parent needs to figure out who's going to manage the behaviors *during* the playdates. It takes a lot of work and can be very taxing on a parent's stress levels.

Parent Caregiver Anxiety

Caregiving for an ASD-diagnosed child is a plate-full, right? Needing to be in constant supervision of your child's life and learning development. Learning the ways in which your child is different from others. Absorbing the fact that how they learn is different, too. Trying to stay two steps ahead of disaster and trying to also run a household and provide a loving home to the rest of the family members. Parents with a child with ASD have to deal with the fact that they are not in full control no matter how hard they work to be. They are facing a journey in which they will encounter a multitude of unknowns. They discover that as soon as they've figured out how to manage one issue, another one—maybe bigger—crops up to replace it. Once they actually define a goal, set it, and accomplish it, a new goal is waiting at the next gate. Sand traps and blind corners are hidden along every turn. Anything can happen anytime.

And that means that anxiety becomes an everyday experience. Without a toolkit of ways to take the edge off the stress, the anxiety, depression, and sometimes anger have nowhere to go but up. Anxiety becomes so persistent and such an overwhelming part of day-to-day life that some parents don't even realize how overwhelmed they are.

Enter Escalating Hypervigilance

Wanting to do their best, parents sometimes dive into trying to learn as much as they can about the diagnosis and about their child's behaviors. They start to realize the scope of the job before them as they learn about treatments and begin to try to coordinate them. They put a lot of pressure on themselves to learn a lot and learn quickly. Unfortunately, there's always more to learn.

Then, as parents wade through the shifting dynamics of their child's young life, many start to think, "I need to be prepared for whatever happens to my child in whatever environment, whether it be school or a social event or an outing. Whatever it takes, I'll do it!" And they begin to get hyper-vigilant, always on the lookout for what might be needed and what might go wrong. They spend an exorbitant amount of time planning, strategizing, and trying to proactively plan the next step to maximize outcomes and minimize disasters. They think that if they can see a problem coming, they can nip it in the bud and avoid problems and outbursts and upsets all around. Hypervigilance becomes their new normal. And the anxiety continues to build.

It's not long before an intense sense of urgency and pressure to get things handled, managed, scheduled, or researched as quickly as possible begins to escalate. With good intentions, parents can't help but conclude that they need to move fast because there's only so much time and so many hours in a day to be able to help their child develop their skills and understanding. Even before the child starts school, they'll think about what they can do to prepare for it. Their child is likely behind academically, and the parents want to get the child "caught up" to their peers as much as possible and as quickly as possible.

As a parent learns more about their child's condition, they begin to recognize triggers in the environment that upset the child, too. They figure that they have to react quickly to avoid a meltdown. They notice that if they are tired and their response isn't quick enough, sometimes harmful behaviors can result. "I can't wait," they think. "The faster I take care of this, the better to avoid that." On top of that, when a parent does have some free time, they end up rushing around trying to get everything else done. There's no real downtime. There's pressure and seemingly not enough hours in the day at every turn.

Everyday worries can become more and more intrusive on the caregiver's ability to function. They always have to be "on." They're always on the lookout for how they can move their child forward, where they might need to prevent outbursts and upsetting behaviors, and what else they need to learn that might be relevant. For parents who have been working diligently to maximize their kid's success, the stress continues to pile on. It doesn't end. Life just gets more and more complex, and as the child celebrates more birthdays, there will always be more to think about, anticipate, and try to help them with.

Making matters worse, as parents push to accomplish as much as possible as quickly as possible, they can have a tremendous fear of seeing any sign of regression in their child. On top of trying to anticipate needs, setting in place proactive strategies to prevent the worst from happening, in the back of their minds, they worry that any delays or loss of progress might be a sign that they are in fact sliding backward and losing some of the skills they've worked so hard to learn. It would be emotionally devastating to them if they couldn't continue to believe that their child is making progress, or they might have to start all over again. It's one more layer of pressure on a stack already piled high.

Locking in Fight/Flight

It's not long before the brains of these overworked parents are deeply into the red zone. They are overtaxed and they begin to feel exhausted—mentally, emotionally, physically, and probably spiritually. All of this urgency and hyper-reactivity puts the brain in that survival "fight or flight" mode, sometimes referred to as "fight/flight/freeze," a phrase associated with Polyvagal Theory. Although there are more "f" states that have been recently added, these are the primary ones I usually see in this population. Essentially, this refers to our brain's reactive mechanisms designed to help us respond to danger as quickly as possible—and survive.

Fight/flight responses are our primal brain's way of protecting us in times of danger; the problem is that we aren't designed to fear danger on an ongoing basis. Our bodies and brains need healthy amounts of decompression time—time to rest, relax, and rejuvenate—in order to be at our best. But the intensity and chronic nature of the stress that caregivers of the ASD population are exposed to is different from stresses in other caregiver groups. It doesn't wax and wane; it easily and quickly can become a constant, long-term engagement. And its chronic nature means the caregiver's brain can stay locked in the fight/flight mode, which it isn't designed to do. The switch is set to On, and it stays there. The caregiver never gets to relax.

The changing attitudes of our culture can put even more of a burden on the parent. Twenty years ago, if a kid had a tantrum or two in school, the school district would get involved. Whether they had a diagnosis or not, they would come up with a plan to deal with the situation. But today, more and more, it appears that unusual or dramatic behaviors are becoming more socially forgiven or acceptable than in the past where they were deemed unacceptable or seen as dangerous. "Yeah, that's just who they are," people say now, and then they move on. Nowadays, schools are challenged with these two seemingly polarized stances on behaviors. They need to decide how much they will get involved and what they can say or do about it if the parent objects. Even though the school can legally take steps, it could get messy. It's another layer of stress for the parent.

Parents can also fool themselves about how much their child is afflicted with the disorder. They might try to focus on their child's great academic skills—they could even be above the other kids academically—but then minimize the fact that their child might not be able to self-regulate through an entire day of school. They might be able to put a sheet of math problems in front of the child, who could finish it faster than anybody. But if the child is shouting out inappropriate scripts all day or if they can't sit still and need to run around all the time, there are significant gaps in their skills that will only be more of a problem as they grow older. Being honest about all facets of the child's strengths and challenges can only empower the parents to help them develop and function as best they can.

As a way of dealing with the stress, parents sometimes try to convince themselves that their child's unusual, disruptive, and sometimes violent behaviors will work themselves out somehow. But they won't. The opposite is true. The sooner those behaviors are recognized for what they are and addressed, the happier everyone will be in the long run.

Getting Adjusted to ABA

As I've mentioned earlier, the ABA model doesn't always exude that warm and fuzzy sheen to it that we've come to associate with childhood learning environments. It's structured and goal-oriented, and while it's well-suited to help those diagnosed, it can sometimes look cold and stiff to the outsider. Getting acquainted with it, understanding how it works, and hopefully, getting more comfortable with it takes time—and that can be challenging and stressful.

Unfortunately, most behaviorists aren't necessarily trained in hand-holding parents through the process; most aren't really trained for the counseling or psychological therapeutic component to assist with parental emotional regulation. A few will go out of their way to help the parents understand this new world they're in, but more often than not, the parents are on their own.

Which, of course, can bring up doubts and concerns in the parents. They might question their course of treatment. They might question if they have the right professional to work with. They might question their own judgment or wonder if they can or should speak up about their concerns. They don't have a frame of reference yet. They might wonder how long of a trial period they should give it before turning elsewhere for direction or answers. While ABA is there to help their child, getting used to it can take a lot of work and energy, and it can take a while—maybe years—for the parents to feel comfortable that they have the right path for their kid. Meanwhile, precious time is going by, and their child needs treatment.

Parents deal with all of this responsibility and overwhelm in different ways. Many families and parents dive into trying to plan ahead for eventualities in order to avoid disaster. A tremendous amount of thought is needed just to make plans to leave the house for almost anything. If there's an upcoming event, they'll spend time thinking through who will be attending, whether they'll be accepted, who might be a problem for the child, and what might trigger the child. Is there someone they have to keep the child away from? If the child has specific needs, the parents pack a bag of special foods or certain reinforcers almost every time they leave the house. Since toilet training is sometimes delayed in this population, it might be necessary to pack diapers, pull-ups, or an extra change of clothes, too. And don't forget medications and/or supplements. Even as kids get a little older, they still might want to pack a bag before leaving the house.

Some parents find themselves in hyper-scheduling mode. If their child is easily overstimulated, quick-moving, and has frequent "meltdowns," they quickly learn to fill the child's schedule with as many things to do as possible. In fact, some behaviorists will coach them to do so, which might be a quick fix in the short run. The reasoning is that many in this population appear to do better with something specific to do, and downtime can be asking for trouble. Unfortunately, while on the surface this might appear to be an appropriate intervention and help relieve stress and reactivity for the child, it can also exacerbate the parents' and the child's hyper-focus on what comes next. They get more tense and more driven to control what happens. I've seen some parents pour an excessive amount of energy into overscheduling activities. The result? At some point, they crash and burn. If we don't teach the child frustration tolerance, flexibility, and temperance, the intervention on its own can be as exhausting as doing nothing.

The Emotional Impact of the Diagnosis

We can't get around the fact that there is an emotional impact to finding out that your child has been diagnosed with an autism spectrum disorder. But, of course, the stress doesn't just begin at diagnosis. The parents have likely been struggling with trying to manage behaviors before then, and other family members and associates might have already been giving them feedback about what they're witnessing.

Actually, the formal diagnosis can bring a sigh of relief for some families. The diagnosis brings something to wrap their heads around and provides a name for the entire range of strange and difficult behaviors. It also implies that many have gone down a similar road before them and that there are people—even experts—out there with experience, insights, and guidance to help them along their unique path. But, once there is a diagnosis, they soon find out that there's a daunting mountain of work in front of them. And the stress can get overwhelming.

Some people find it hard to face the shock and disappointment of the diagnosis, so they deal with stress and overwhelm by shielding themselves from the facts of the situation and ignoring them. They don't know there are better options, so they do the best they can with it. But if parents don't face the developmental delays in their child honestly and they don't initiate service or get treatment for them, they only make matters worse for themselves in the future.

Much more than with previous generations, I find that today's parents sometimes don't recognize that their child's problematic behaviors will only get worse later in life if they don't address them early enough. Society is now so much more accepting of behaviors that fall outside of what was once considered the "norm" than it has ever been— and that's a good thing for the most part. But when it comes to diagnosed kids, I've seen more and more parents demonstrate a passive response. Sure, it's a big ask. To be ready to deal with and face all the unknowns involved with the diagnosis. But avoidance or denial won't help. It only delays the child's access to the treatment they need.

In addition to the mounting anxiety they feel since they learned of the diagnosis, parents of a child with ASD can experience many more emotions. A lot of repressed or overt anger and resentment can arise when the child is still young. The parent might wonder about the child's potential and worry that their hopes and dreams for the child might not actually be fulfilled. There can be a lot of grief and feelings of loss, too, as the parent deals with letting go of those hopes and dreams. And many feel angry about being unable to meet their child's needs as well as they want to, thinking that they should be able to.

When parents are taking their first steps to deal with the diagnosis and providers hand them a list of resources for treatment, parents often dare to be hopeful. But what at first seems like a treasure trove of answers can end up being a Pandora's box of more and more questions. Resources, access to them, and the ways in which they are funded can vary greatly from one area to the next. There are a lot of decisions to make. As they begin to learn about what services their child might need and which ones are available, and as they try to make decisions about what is best for their child, parents get even more overwhelmed.

They might be looking for the next kind of supplemental treatment, such as those provided by specialized physicians and specialists that manage coexisting disorders, diet, or other physical health issues that so often accompany the ASD diagnosis and rely solely on those interventions with high hopes. Besides turning to behavioral therapy as a treatment modality, professionals might recommend auxiliary therapies, even at the time the diagnosis is first made. Speech therapy is very helpful even if the child can speak in full sentences or appears to be learning words. For the record, I highly recommend as much speech therapy as clinically appropriate at a young age—even as a toddler. Communication development is so much more than just speaking words; getting started early puts them in front of the curve. Private outpatient speech therapy can be sought in early years and can continue likely with insurance coverage.

Adding to a parent's concerns, some medical interventions can be very costly to maintain and typically aren't covered by insurance. Parents might be pleased that they've found hope for progress but worry if they'll be able to afford it long-term.

Kids with ASD also frequently require physical and/or occupational therapy. If it's clinically warranted, they can receive these therapies in an outpatient setting, too. Parents need to seek out an evaluation or consultation to assess the need.

More parents are finding information online about some of the newer, more experimental treatments—and many people seem to have strong feelings one way or the other about them. The competing and often disagreeing voices found through online searches add just one more layer of stress to parents as they try to make decisions about what treatments to set up for the child. They can sometimes leave the parent more confused than when they started. It can be extremely time-consuming and exhausting to add other types of treatment to the puzzle.

Facing the diagnosis, having to try new things, and adding to fit in one more piece to an already-full puzzle can be grueling. Doubts, worries, fears creep in easily, readily, frequently. Their heads feel like they're spinning, and they sometimes don't know which way is up. "Stressful" is an understatement.

And There's More

Having a child with ASD can affect virtually all areas of a parent's life, directly or indirectly. Not surprisingly, because of the high levels of stress, it's not uncommon for spouses to encounter significant disagreements. Maintaining a strong marriage or co-parenting partnership is difficult enough, but when you add to the mix the need to manage a child with a variety of intense and demanding needs, it can take a substantial toll on the marriage.

Any existing marital issues often intensify during this period because both parents are facing challenging questions. Add to that having opposing views on what should be done, when it should be done, or even *if* it should be done adds fuel to the fire. If one parent is accepting and ready to dive into treatment and the other is in denial, it can add even more strain on each parent—as well as place a confusing set of expectations on the child.

Babysitters and caregiver help would provide a much-needed occasional respite from the demands of the caregiver "job," but it can be quite difficult to find someone to do so. Parents might not have the resources to pay someone to watch their child safely, and family members might not understand how to care for the child, or they might be unwilling to. This lack of caregiving help can be exhausting at any stage.

Spiritual questioning can come up, too, as so many aspects of life seem to be bucking all at the same time. Parents sometimes question their faith and beliefs that they've had for many years. And because of all the time they're investing in their child's well-being, they might not be able to attend spiritual functions as much as they had in the past. In turn, that can bring about a greater sense of isolation from their peers and distance them from their faith and their sense of community. Sometimes faith-based institutions have childcare, but often the diagnosed kids can be outside of the caregiver's expertise to manage safely.

Isolation becomes a bigger issue when they find themselves passing up social opportunities in order to invest the time needed to address the unique needs of their child. That might be compounded if they start getting passed over when invitations are sent out or if they're asked not to participate in an event if they can't ensure their child's behavior will be appropriate and safe. If their friends, family, or community isn't honest about any worries or feelings they're having, the parents often can still sense their judgment of their family and feel hurt and rejected because of it.

Stressing over Interventions

Another stressor for parents with school-age children has to do with interacting with interventions. It used to seem more common for children to first be diagnosed around school age, but thanks to increased ASD awareness these days, it has become more common for a child to be evaluated for early intervention services from birth to age three.

The earlier the intervention, the better the prognosis. It also helps the parent learn the ropes and ease themselves more gradually into what may become more intensive treatment to come in the years ahead.

If the child hasn't been referred for an Individualized Education Plan or Program (IEP) before school age through early intervention services, the school might initiate the IEP process if the child is exhibiting concerning behaviors in the first few months of their attendance. They'd sit down together and talk about starting an IEP process and what that might look like. Then they'd gather a team of school staff to create the IEP, start a full evaluation and assessment process—using FBA methodologies—and then put together the IEP's academic plan and behavioral plan.

Once the evaluation has been completed, the teachers and the team at school meet with the parents to review these preliminary assessment results and discuss what they've learned about their child and how they might better support them. This first IEP meeting can be overwhelming to parents. If they were expecting to just send their child off to school and think that their work was done, they are in for a rude and stressful surprise. The IEP assessment also typically includes the child's Intelligent Quotient (IQ), which can be shocking to some parents when they find out their child isn't the genius they thought they were.

At the meeting, parents are typically presented with an evaluation summary and tentative plan that looks like the size of a booklet that reveals all the reports, statistics, scores, assessments, and other things that contribute to the assessment. It will also list the goals and provide a set of plans to reach those goals for the child.

On top of that, the school asks the parents for their opinions about the plans and goals. Are there any changes they want to make? For the first few years, the parents can feel so overwhelmed and outnumbered that they say very little. But by the time the child finishes high school, I often see the parent leading those meetings!

Then, as parents and school staff monitor the child's progress over time, they will re-evaluate from time to time whether or not the child is making enough progress in the school setting. They might review the child's need for intensive support or whether they should be referred to outside placement. They could consider a licensed private school, a school that specializes in autism spectrum disorder, or they might mix and match half days of school with half days in an autistic support classroom within the school district. They might even consider other creative ways to meet the child's academic needs. Having so many options for individualized and specialized placement can be scary for parents; sometimes, they fear that their child might pick up poor behaviors from other kids. Again, all the choices can be agonizing to deal with.

Parents can also experience some trauma as they leave their child with other professionals, especially before the child has developed a reliable set of communication skills. They might feel that the professionals initially put the child in more distress instead of reducing it. And they might continue to harbor concerns about providers for years to come.

Learning to work with and master the IEP process through the years can be one more distressing dimension. This continues through the high school years as the focus shifts to pre-vocational planning and transition services. Parents need to work with the IEP team to devise their child's development plan, learn their rights, and learn how to advocate for their child. It is a job they'll have throughout their child's educational career.

Dealing with the Public

Parents of ASD-diagnosed kids often get anxious when they think about interacting with the public with their child. They might be concerned about the public's perceptions, wondering if people will misunderstand the reason for their child's behavior. Many struggle with the question of whether or not they should even reveal the diagnosis or just deal with the embarrassment and the assumptions being made about them.

The family's ability to attend structured religious services has to be re-examined, as well. They'd have to decide if the child's behavior might be too disruptive to maintain through a service. When the service gets quiet, members of the congregation can sometimes feel that their right to worship has been infringed upon if the child persistently engages in unsettling behaviors. Thankfully, there are many religious institutions that are very welcoming and accepting of children with special needs and accommodate their service providers.

In the back of most parents' minds is also a concern that, when they're out in public, someone might misinterpret their child's behavior—or the parent's response to it—and report it. Maladaptive and inappropriate behaviors towards strangers can be shocking and disturbing to the public. A diagnosed child might run over to strangers and touch them inappropriately or cause some property damage in stores. It might be difficult for a diagnosed child not to grab things off the shelves. Constant supervision is required of the parents to make sure these things don't happen.

To make matters worse, people have on occasion contacted Child Protective Services after witnessing a situation that they completely misunderstood. In Pennsylvania, Childline is a state-wide call-in child protective service funded by the Department of Human Services to prevent and disrupt child abuse. Unfortunately, when I was working in Pennsylvania, I found that people would occasionally submit reports to Childline, making erroneous judgments about what they had witnessed. This was largely attributed to the fact that they weren't familiar with how severe and dramatic the behaviors of the ASD population can be and didn't understand the use of the behavior modification methods that were being used to try to de-escalate the child. No parent wants to have social services knocking at their door when they were doing their best to respond to an unwanted and unexpected display in public.

• • • • •

How, then, can a caregiver manage to be responsible, effective, caring, knowledgeable, and compassionate, all at the same time? How do they do this without getting completely snowed under by all of the tremendously stress-inducing reality of raising a child with ASD? How can a parent still attend to their own health and well-being while managing the behaviors and development of their ASD-diagnosed child? How can they stay healthy and resilient? In the next chapter, I'll introduce you to energy psychology techniques and show you why they make so much sense for caregivers—helping them boost skills, improve decision-making, and understand how they can stay healthy in the midst of everything.

6

Energy Psychology

When I was working at Highlands Hospital Regional Center for Autism, I was very pleased to see how skilled and professional my staff were at their jobs, especially those in the licensed private school division. After the school day ended and the students left, the next part of their day included gathering in a room together to discuss the children and compile data about their progress and prepare individualized curricula for the following day. Since there were video cameras in each of the school rooms, I could occasionally check in on how the staff's day was winding down with a glance at the video feed displayed on monitors in my office. One afternoon, I returned to my office and glanced over at the screens to get a sense of how they were doing after a long day. Their body language communicated a lot to me. I was surprised at what I saw because, on the one hand, I knew how deeply devoted to their work they were. Yet they looked tired, frustrated, and a little ticked off. So, I went into the room to see what I could find out.

I asked them how everything was going, and—true to their professional nature—they responded, "Fine! Everything's good!" So I let it go.

The next day, the same thing happened. I could tell from the video feed that my staff was not "fine" at all. When I went to check in with them again, and again they responded that things were okay. But I didn't buy it this time.

"I don't believe you," I told them. "Listen. I want to remind you that I have a bunch of tools—energy psychology tools—that I find quite effective. So, if something's going on with you, let me know, and maybe we can do something about it."

Over the year, I had given them a few structured training sessions to introduce them to some energy psychology techniques, per their requests. They weren't to use them with the kids in the program; the intent was to broaden my staff's exposure to a variety of methods because they expressed interest in expanding their scope of learning.

One of them let out a loud sigh. "You know, I love my job, and I love being here," she said, "but I go home, and I'm just irritable. I can't keep it together around my significant other or my kids. The truth is, well, I'm exhausted."

I completely got it. The hiring standards my staff had to live up to were incredibly high. They had excellent clinical skillsets in applied behavior analysis. In their work environment, working with people with autism spectrum disorder, unexpected, dangerous, destructive, and other maladaptive behaviors can erupt out of nowhere. They needed to have the fortitude and presence of mind to remain neutral in those escalated situations, make pivotal decisions really quickly, and maintain a certain level of energy all day long to keep up the learning momentum—all of which can be very taxing. It was understandable why they were feeling the way they did.

"Okay," I told them. "Let me think about this and come up with a game plan."

I called my consultant. "I know that anything having to do with energy psychology is off-limits for the kids in the program. It's an ABA program, after all," I told him. "But I'm wondering if you're opposed to me helping the staff manage their own stress with EP tools?" He agreed. Then I had another lightbulb idea. If I provide them with an EP-based tool, I could also do an informal study on the outcomes of my staff's progress with the help of energy psychology and measure their stress levels before and after their use of the EP technique. After all, if it was successful shouldn't everyone have the tools?

I came up with a brief baseline study using a Likert scale, a rating system for people to rate their level of agreement to a statement from "Strongly Disagree" to "Strongly Agree" to be administered prior the intervention. Consisting of a few simple questions about their quality of work life and home life, and filled out anonymously, the survey would help me measure each staff person's stress levels. I gave each of them the survey to fill out, and then, three times a day, they were to do the EP technique I taught them—twice at work and once at home. It was a simple breathing exercise that takes just two minutes to do. Most of the staff participated in the study and did the exercises as I instructed for eight weeks. When they were done, I gave them the same rating scale to fill out all over again.

Once they all had completed and submitted their post-study survey, I sat down with them and asked them to share with me about their experiences using the EP technique. They reported that over those eight weeks, they had felt more energized and found it easier to rebalance themselves after tough situations arose. They were more resilient and felt calmer and more centered. As they were doing the exercise, they said, they could feel their body shifting, their tension lessening, and even observed their thoughts slowing down—generally achieving a greater sense of calm by the time they were done. Most of them also expressed feeling that their work on the job had improved, and remember, these were already superstars at work!

But there was another surprising benefit, as well. The breathing exercise I gave them is designed to address all four quadrants of the brain: top, bottom, left, and right. After they had been doing it for a while, many developed an ability to notice when their stress levels were starting to creep up throughout the day. And since they couldn't just excuse themselves from whatever they were doing to take two minutes to do the breathing exercise, they could take a more traditional approach from Cognitive Behavioral Therapy (CBT) to help turn things back around. That is, they'd stop the thought they were having mid-stream and remind themselves not to go down that rabbit hole. "I don't care about dinner," they might choose to think to themselves. "I don't care if my husband's mad at me. Let me come back, regroup, and be present."

The breathing technique helped them get some sort of internal alert when they started physically entering a sort of yellow zone, and, with some self-intervention, they could stop it from getting worse. They even came up with a term for this new superpower: "flipping the switch." With the newfound awareness, they could rein in their stress and de-escalate from within.

From an energy psychology standpoint, it's believed that this process is not just cognitive; it involves a complex interplay between physiology and psychology. It's why it's not enough to just say to yourself, "Hey, I'm headed towards yellow," and that would be enough to get you to stop, take a deep breath, and take time to de-stress. It's also why self-talk is rarely enough to effect long-term change.

That awareness is golden; most people live in a state of at least some low-grade chronic stress and don't recognize those times when the stress levels escalate further—until it's too late. Lots of people teeter on that edge of what they believe to be good, alert functioning, and being over-stressed. But many energy psychology tools can be used for basic stress management, helping to buy you time before going from 0 to 100 in a situation. After using EP strategies for a while, I find the relationship between the mind and body improves, making traditional self-talk easier and more accessible to assist in maintaining calm.

I chose the particular breathing exercise to give to my staff because I find it gets the most bang for the buck for most people who do not exhibit clinically complex issues. It takes just two minutes, which seems a crazy, implausibly short time to invest in this exercise, but it builds that "flipping-the-switch" superpower. The trick is that you are physically sending signals to your brain to calm the body, and you also learn what that process *feels* like. That helps you build confidence that it *can* be done quickly and consistently, and you don't even need any external tools to do it. With this technique—which I share with you below—you can learn to calm yourself down and self-regulate much more quickly than even other EP methods; I find it to be one of the simplest foundational tools. Of course, other energy psychology techniques might be required to address the layers of any problem that inevitably come with more complicated issues. But for general stress, it is a wonderful little tool in the methods of energy psychology.

The survey results, too, underscored the impressive improvement in the staff's sense of efficacy, responsiveness, and resilience. All of the staff had improved to some degree on almost every item. While I hadn't really initiated the study for research purposes—the goal was to help my staff become more resilient in their stressful jobs—and this practice revealed some very valuable indicators. It was published in the *International Journal of Healing and Caring.*[10]

Later, going over the results of the study, another big lightbulb lit up for me.

I knew that parents and caregivers of those with ASD desperately need tools like this to prevent burnout and exhaustion. Parents/caregivers of those with ASD have little choice but to be subjected to a barrage of stress and anxiety, as I've discussed in depth in the last chapter. Their hypervigilant fight/flight brain gets stuck in the On position—and that is not sustainable. Not only is it not good for you, the caregiver, but if you're burnt out and exhausted, you can hardly do anybody else any good either. That light bulb was telling me something important.

EP Goes Mainstream

I consider myself very fortunate to have met Dr. Nicosia early in my career and, through him, to be introduced to energy psychology techniques and the tremendous difference they can make in people's lives. His practice often attracted patients who were on the verge of losing all hope about being able to turn around devastating health conditions. Many had significant pain and were on potent medications, and many were told by the medical community that nothing more could be done for them. Many patients had experienced multiple surgeries; they'd had cancer return again and again, or had debilitating pain that affected every aspect of their lives. Others had very complex, multi-layered conditions. Yet, the clinical staff at Advanced Diagnostics taught them the most innovative energy psychology tools at that time and instructed them to do

---

10 Freger, M. (2019). Use of over energy correction (OEC) for intervention therapists at a center-based treatment facility for autism spectrum disorders (ASD). International Journal of Healing and Caring, 19(2). https://www.ijhc.org/use-of-over-energy-correction-oec-for-intervention-therapists-at-a-center-based-treatment-facility-for-autism-spectrum-disorders-asd-freger

them frequently throughout the day. I saw people's pain levels decrease significantly. I saw many who, with their doctors' approval, were able to reduce some of the medications they were on. I saw people get on track with sleep issues, among other things, and their overall quality of life vastly improved. By applying a few energy psychology techniques, I even helped one young woman who was addicted to heroin completely turn around a reportedly unbearable experience of withdrawal. Practicing this stuff makes a difference in a wide variety of ways.

How does it work? Energy psychology uses the body's bio-energetic system to tap into the mind-body connection. Our thoughts can influence our bodily sensations —what can be called "top-down communication"—and the body can send signals back up to the brain and make us feel a certain way—"bottom-up" communication. The health of both pathways is essential for clear communication and functioning. So, when we experience stress or pain or something disruptive, we want to be detectives and get to the root of that disruption and find out what's really going on.

EP helps to shift the flow of information and energy in the body and its energy field. Some of the most popular energy psychology methods used today are the Emotional Freedom Techniques (EFT), Thought Field Therapy (TFT), Comprehensive Energy Psychology (CEP), Eye Movement Desensitization and Reprocessing (EMDR), Tapas Acupressure Technique (TAT), Heart Assisted Therapy (HAT) and Advanced Integrative Therapy (AIT), just to name a few. They are each designed to strategically intervene with human energy fields in order to boost physical, mental, emotional, and spiritual well-being. Practitioners who employ energy psychology include psychotherapists, counselors, coaches, energy healers, and others, respective of their scope of practice.

EP techniques help the traumas and issues trapped in the body to come out. Past stressors can accumulate and snowball, so working on them can require attention to multiple layers of traumas or upsets that end up tying into the present concern. Unlike traditional talk therapy, where therapists and patients discuss and investigate a trauma over and over again, using traditionally slower tools, energy psychology helps the patient address the issues at the root. By addressing the body, it's amazing how quickly the thoughts and feelings around an issue can change. Over several sessions, EP methods often safely and gently help uncover buried psychological issues that drive discomfort and unhappiness—and more importantly, often release and heal them.

Dr. Nicosia had taught me TEST™—which is his offshoot of Thought Field Therapy. I found that when I work with people, I first like to build a foundation by doing a breathing exercise like the one I did in the study. Then I often like to teach aspects of TFT and EFT (sometimes called "tapping," EFT is a simplified version of Thought Field Therapy) to people so they can experience and understand how their body feels when it starts to de-escalate.

One thing I appreciate most about energy psychology is that you never have to risk getting stuck in "analysis paralysis" as you try to figure things out. For example, if someone has chronic stomachaches and their doctor has ruled out and physical causes, the logical next step might be to conclude that the problem must be stress related. In fact, the physician will likely suggest that when they have ruled out medical issues. But, if you ask the person, they might say they don't know what they're stressed about. To the energy psychology practitioner, that's OK. The client doesn't have to know that level of detail for them to be able to get results. Energy psychology techniques give us tools to work through issues without even having all the answers in front of us. As a result, much more can get done.

Over the years, I have introduced concepts of energy psychology to quite a few ABA therapists and found most of them responded with a sigh of relief. They, like me, felt that it was the missing piece, allowing practitioners to help people address feelings and emotions that naturally come up.

Here's how the Association for Comprehensive Energy Psychology (ACEP) defines energy psychology on their website (https://www.energy psych.org/energy-psychology).

Energy psychology, also known as cognitive somatic practices, comprises a family of mind-body methods designed to strategically and methodically intervene with human energy fields in elevating physical, mental, emotional and spiritual well-being.

Energy psychology (EP) methods combine cognitive interventions with somatic techniques that influence the human bio-energy systems such as meridians, chakras and the biofield, as well as subtler systems of the body such as neuroception. Activation of these systems during the intervention is thought to increase the speed and/or thoroughness of the work.

These approaches are used by practitioners of psychotherapy, counseling, coaching, energy healing, and health optimization.

Practitioners view symptoms as systemic, interactive bio-energetic patterns. This involves constant complex communication among neurobiological processes, electrophysiology, consciousness, and bioenergy systems. Energy psychology (EP) helps people shift the flow of information and energy throughout these systems to facilitate healing and growth.

Most EP approaches are brief, active and structured. EP approaches can be: 1) used as stand-alone interventions, and 2) easily integrated within a broader clinical treatment, program of change or health optimization. Clients also learn self-help techniques they can use themselves.

EP approaches are often rapid, have little to no adverse effects, and are usually experienced as self-empowering by clients and patients.

Thanks in part to ACEP's in-depth research library on energy psychology, its comprehensive trainings, and its drive to encourage research in the field, The American Psychological Association has given ACEP the honor of including continuing education credits for approved courses in evidence-based EP course offerings. Having a mainstream organization do the research and give its approval to an emerging methodology such as EP marked a significant turning point for energy psychology; it no longer was relegated to being too "weird" to be acceptable.

Energy psychology is also supported by the work and research of William Tiller, PhD, professor emeritus of materials science and engineering at Stanford University, geochemist Walter E. Dibble, Jr., PhD, and Michael J. Kohane, PhD, who together authored *Conscious Acts of Creation: The Emergence of a New Physics*. While the book covers a wide scope of topics, it drives home the science behind the idea that we humans are made up of more than just our skin and bones. The authors present the science behind the idea that all humans have "bio bodysuits," or energy fields that intermingle with our physical bodies and, where our thoughts and feelings contribute to this, extending beyond our physical body by some feet. The works of Thornton Streeter, Beverly Rubick, and Shamini Jain have also supported the idea of the biofield of the human body and have demonstrated similar results. Dr. Rick Leskowitz recently contributed to the field of EP with his article, "A Cartography of Energy Medicine: From Subtle Anatomy to Energy Physiology," which is an excellent overview of what we think we know so far.[11]

The authors also discuss how our thoughts and emotions affect our energy fields, which is an integral aspect of EP philosophy. It is an idea that can bring us much greater skill as caregivers, and I discuss it in depth in the next chapter. Changing our perceptions can powerfully bring about changes in our life experiences and can help to rewire the brain. These are valuable insights when we want to change our own behaviors and reactions.

Finally, I do want to emphasize that if a practitioner wants to treat clinical mental health disorders with energy psychology techniques, they need to possess a clinical designation or license. Just because a professional uses energy psychology techniques, they are not necessarily licensed psychologists; they are simply energy psychology practitioners. In other words, just because someone is experienced with the techniques and has the ability to practice energy psychology techniques doesn't automatically mean that they are qualified to treat clinical mental health issues defined in the DSM-V. One should hold a specific, approved license, such as psychiatry, psychology, counseling, or social work, to do so.

---

11 Leskowitz E. A cartography of energy medicine: From subtle anatomy to energy physiology. Explore (NY). 2022 Mar–Apr;18(2):15–164. doi: 10.1016/j.explore.2020.09.008. Epub 2020 Sep 25. PMID: 33168457.

◆ ◆ ◆ ◆ ◆

By folding in some simple energy psychology practices into their lives, parents and other caregivers of kids with ASD have a secret weapon to help them take the edge off of stress and to recenter and reclaim their energy. But that, by itself, is not enough to sustain an energized life for the long term. In the next chapter, I'll talk about three components of effectiveness, which, if optimized, will help you manage, monitor, enhance, and stabilize your resilience and vitality so you can feel full of life again.

7

Being Effective as a Caregiver and Energized as a Human Being

As I've discussed in preceding chapters, being a parent and/or caregiver of a person with an autism spectrum disorder can be an extraordinarily demanding job. For that reason, burnout is common—and can be terribly destructive, despite one's good intentions. Burnout undermines your ability to make decisions, hinders your ability to successfully respond to emerging destructive behaviors in the present, and sabotages your attempts to plan and strategize for success in the future. Burnout doesn't only interfere with your effectiveness; it drags down your confidence and weakens the impact you have in the moment. And just as importantly—if not more so—burnout can affect your health and your ability to take care of yourself and thrive in your life. If it gets too bad, you're not much better than a wet noodle, doing no one any good at all. It's the bane of caregiver existence.

So how do we avoid burnout? How can we prevent it—or reverse it if we're already circling the drain? How can we stay balanced as we endure the burdens of caregiving as we constantly deal with unexpected, maladaptive behaviors, learn the new language and practices of ABA, plan and collaborate on developmental and educational strategies, deal with changes to social interactions, plan, schedule, prepare, learn—and also be there for someone we love, every day?

To help people get a handle on how they can better manage it all and still be at their best, I've broken things down into what I consider to be the three components of effectiveness for caregivers of people with

ASD. These are: your skills, your will, and your biofield strength. Let's take these one at a time.

Your *skills* consist of whatever set of skills you've accumulated and also reflects your knowledge of the interventions that are best to treat the symptoms of your child's diagnosis.

Your *will*, of course, is your willingness to do the work, to carry out the interventions, and to get in and stay in the ring.

The *biofield* is another term for what Dr. Tiller and his co-authors call the "bio bodysuit." The concept first arose in embryology in 1912 to explain the embryo's developmental process, but it has grown to encompass information delivery within the body. The term has been accepted as a Medical Subject Heading (MeSH) at the National Library of Medicine, and all practitioners that deal with energy psychology or energy healing engage with it. While the biofield is most often described as being electromagnetic in nature, some have proposed that it involves quantum information flow, as well. It may not be visible to the human eye, but countless studies have been done on it throughout the last century.

In their 2015 paper, "Biofield Science and Healing: History, Terminology and Concepts," Beverly Rubik, PhD, David Muesham, PhD, Richard Hammerschlag, PhD, and Shamini Jain, PhD, describe the biofield this way:

> The biofield or biological field, a complex organizing energy field engaged in the generation, maintenance, and regulation of biological homeodynamics, is a useful concept that provides the rudiments of a scientific foundation for energy medicine and thereby advances the research and practice of it.[12]

Your level of skills, your degree of will, and the strength of your biofield affect each other, as you'll see. When all of them are optimized, you'll find yourself much more sustainably resilient, effective, clear-headed, and healthy for the long term.

---

12 Rubik, B., Muehsam, D., Hammerschlag, R., & Jain, S. (2015). Biofield Science and Healing: History, Terminology, and Concepts. Global advances in health and medicine, 4(Suppl), 8–14. https://doi.org/10.7453/gahmj.2015.038.suppl

Skills

For caregivers of kids with ASD, growing your skill means learning more about it and acquiring a toolbox of scientifically reputable techniques under the ABA umbrella that work for you and the child. Caregiver skill levels can range from very low—having a profound lack of learned abilities—to very high—having a mastery of a wide range of methods and approaches they can use with success. And even if one's toolbox of techniques seems pretty full, there will always be gaps in learning or techniques since your child's skills evolve, and there's always more to learn.

But in addition to reflecting how many ABA techniques you've got under your belt, your skill level also reflects your ability to choose among the techniques you've learned and apply the most appropriate and fitting one to get the best results. In other words, it's not just about how full your toolbox is; it's how well you can apply them in the moment. I like to refer to this as the *art* of using ABA. Can you make the best choices for intervention in the moment? Can you be flexible when whatever you've tried doesn't get you the response you were looking for from your child, and you have to try another one or wait that one out? Over time, you can collect a whole array of methods and approaches, each of which might seem equally as effective. You have choices to make, and the better the choices, the more skilled you become.

Unfortunately, those layers and layers of stress and anxiety that are normal and expected for caregivers—as discussed in the last few chapters—put most people into their emotionally reactive, fight/flight mindset, which is rarely useful when trying to make the best decisions in tense situations. In fact, emotional reactivity clouds good judgment and sabotages best practices. That's why I like to point out that one of the most important skills you can have as a caregiver, beyond ABA skills, is *emotional regulation*—the ability to manage your own emotional state and choose to stay logical rather than emotional.

When a caregiver can't yet rely on a solid toolbox of skills, and when the "mud" hits the fan, they often fall back on reacting emotionally and making choices and decisions from their feelings. But decisions made that way will rarely be as clear and successful as those we make when we call on whatever skills we have learned and then use our logical, rational left-brain to guide our decision-making. Even those who feel a calling as a behavior specialist can launch into anger or upset when they don't get the responses they're seeking from a child from time to time if they haven't mastered emotional regulation.

But emotional responses will only backfire when we're caregiving. Our emotionally-charged responses—often our attempt to overcompensate for feeling powerless—can come across as aggression to others and make people defensive and uncooperative—which is the opposite of what we want. In other words, actions we take from our unpleasant emotions don't get us the results we're hoping to get.

The ability to manage your emotional responses becomes an incredibly important skill that will directly affect how successful you are at calming or teaching your child.

Finally, the power of ABA can be had even with a basic level of skill. If you remember, ABA is built on the model of antecedent-behavior-consequence (ABC) to help us as caregivers to understand and change maladaptive behaviors in those we care for. For parents, it's important to focus on that first component—the antecedent—to make sure that the child is set up as best as possible for successful behavior change. This begins with the skill of using the "three C's" in our directives: being "clear, concise, and consistent" with our communication. That means we make sure that we have their attention first, that we're physically close to them when we talk with them, and if they're in another room, we don't assume that if we yell at them, they can hear us and process what we said. For example, we don't try to give them a directive if they're staring at the TV, or we get in front of the TV if we have to in order to get their attention. You might not have extensive ABA program knowledge about what to teach your child, but if you start with simple directives using the three C's, you can do quite a lot. They are a huge part of ABA for a reason.

Will

It's not surprising that will is an important factor of effectiveness. We all know that when someone wants to do something, they usually do it better and probably more efficiently than someone that doesn't want to do it. Employee performance management studies have explored attributes of the willingness to do something for many years. Most are derived from Paul Hersey and Ken Blanchard's work in 1969 and were renamed the "Situational Leadership Model" in the mid-1970s. In their research, they rate the employee's "will" in part according to the employee's level of involvement and the extent to which they are risk tolerant. Having some tolerance for risk is necessary as a caregiver of someone with ASD since they need to be willing to expose themselves to new ideas and try their hands at new methods.

But when it comes to parents and other caregivers of those with ASD, will has to do with their willingness to work with the person needing care in the first place. That, of course, isn't something you can just go out and study and become more proficient in. It's the elephant in the room, really, because at some point, a lot of parents just want to give up. They're so tired, but they can't admit it. It's their child, and they "want to want to do the work." Still, will is a factor in how effective a caregiver can be, so it's important to take a good hard look at what level of willingness one truly has to do the work.

Being willing to do something is not quite the same as desiring to do something. As we've all experienced at one time or another, there are sometimes things that we really don't *want* to do, but we're still *willing* to do them. Desire, on the other hand, has to do with how much your heart is driving your passion to do what you do. Professional caregivers usually have a strong desire, and their will is high because they often feel that they were born to work with and help those they care for. It resonates for them. Having that kind of desire to do something usually energizes one's will, so, ideally, we have both.

Another factor that can increase your willingness is the need to do something just to survive. We're willing to do certain things when we have to, for example, if we're under financial, emotional, social, or other pressures. Case in point: parents are usually willing to do whatever they need to help their child survive.

But your willingness can plummet when life circumstances make the job or the tasks less doable or less enjoyable—perhaps when your job changes or your personal life gets more demanding—especially over time. At that time, desire might be non-existent, but flickers of willingness might still keep you showing up every day to get the job done.

The Biofield

If your biofield is healthy and strong, it gives you both emotional and psychological resilience to the ups and downs you face in life, and it supports your ability to be present and fully functional in the moment. When it's strong, you feel energetic yet centered, calm, present, and resourceful. From that state, if you have to make tough decisions, you can do so more consciously and confidently, and the outcomes are usually much more successful.

The paper by Rubik and her colleagues describes in-depth the physiological and biochemical factors that affect the human biofield. But our thoughts and feelings also contribute to our overall field strength. So, people's biofield strength can range from very low to quite high. While most behaviorists and practitioners don't have the means to physically measure the strength of a person's biofield in a tangible way, they can dialog and get a subjective self-report from them to learn about their resilience and confidence. They can look at what behaviors can change or what they might do with best practices.

When we have what I call "low biofield strength," we have greater permeability with the environment and all that's going on around us; we drain easily, and we simply feel zapped of energy. With what I call "high biofield strength," we feel centered, resilient, and able to focus and resist draining distractions. We feel replenished; we feel like we can get things accomplished. The biofield can be thought of as the engine behind all the learning we do to build our skill level as well as our passion, motivation, and will. That is why maintaining a caregiver's energy field is so directly critical to their well-being and, indirectly, the well-being of those they care for.

Have you ever seen people that just have some sort of effect on the people around them that you can't put your finger on? They have something intangible, not behavioral, that calms people down, for example, for no observable reason. You wonder: Is it just because they seem "centered"? It's a sure sign that the person has a strong, resilient biofield, at least at that given moment.

As the biofield becomes stronger and more resilient, shifts in consciousness will occur for the better, which can influence others. Kids are sensitive to that influence, too, even if they don't know it. This is a key piece that I talk to caregivers about: As a person working to help change behaviors of someone with ASD, being centered can be a potent force working for you. I've seen some parents who'd been adopting methods to rebuild their resiliency find some of their child's difficult behaviors dissolve much more readily. Of course, I can't promise anything. But I have seen it happen a number of times.

I work with sports teams, and a coach recently asked me about this dynamic.

"Here's a question for you," she said. "If seven of my team members get on board with strengthening their energy field like you're saying, but two of them don't, are those two going to bring the team down or hold them back?" I told her that the seven would help lift the rest of the team. There's power in numbers, I said, and those seven girls will be a force. Since their fields are stronger, they *might* be more likely to have more focus and be less susceptible to outside influence.

Now, like almost everything else having to do with human beings, energy fields come in different sizes and shapes. Still, while people practicing energy psychology techniques usually have a basic understanding of the biofield as well as direct experience with it, they don't exactly greet people in their offices by saying, "Hi. Let me measure your field so I know where it is today!" There are some studies that show that the strength of a person's biofield corresponds to its size; strong biofields are often larger while the person exhibits more of a presence. And even though we can't see it with our physical eyes, we often sense that it's there. Some people can walk into a room, and you can just feel them 20 feet away. They just have a presence. That's a strong field.

On the other hand, some people have such small fields that they can virtually disappear in a room. And because we can't see someone's field, we don't know what we're interacting with. Sure, many of us do get gut feelings or intuitions about other people's fields, but unfortunately most of us have conditioned ourselves to block out that information source because of cultural norms or not having the tools to accurately interpret it. We might even subtly notice nonverbal cues like gestures and body language, but we still fall back on relying on focusing on the words people speak—and everything else fades away. Again, what factors actually contribute to the biofield strength are complex and still being scientifically studied.

All this is helpful to us as caregivers if we keep in mind that when we're around other people, we never really know what energy they're bringing with them or what we're inevitably interacting with on very subtle levels. We don't know what resilience our field needs or what it might be up against.

There is growing evidence of another characteristic of biofields— they affect and are affected by our thoughts and emotions. In *Conscious Acts of Creation: The Emergence of a New Physics*, the authors describe how that works. Specifically, negative thoughts can weaken biofields, and positive, loving thoughts can help make the biofield more resilient. I've come to associate a strong and resilient biofield with two important qualities in a caregiver: assertiveness and confidence.

Generally, assertiveness has a low emotional charge; it is clear-headed, informed action based on logic and experience. When we're assertive, we draw from our growing set of skills and the knowledge we've gathered, and we make our best judgment calls. For that reason, the effort we put in results in success more of the time than if we just fall back on reacting emotionally—which inevitably activates the fight/flight mechanism. If we're angry, we'll likely go into fight mode. If our emotion is predominantly sadness or helplessness, we'll likely withdraw or remove ourselves from the situation. If we're overwhelmed, we'll probably freeze. If we're frustrated, we might ignore the situation as best we can. If we're uncomfortable, we might change the subject and try to avoid it. All of these ineffective responses to emotions are going to lead us to make poorer decisions and get poorer outcomes. And when doubt or fear starts to take over, the air goes out of the balloon, the biofield likely weakens, and our assertiveness goes out the window.

Lack of confidence affects the biofield, too. When someone feels like they don't know what they're doing, they can have thoughts that spiral their energy downward. "Oh jeez, I don't have a clue here. Am I screwing up, or, worse, am I causing harm?" Anxiety or frustration can set in. If we're emotionally charged, it's never a good time to make decisions. In other words, if we're in an emotional state, we're at risk of making emotionally driven choices, and that means we'll be more prone to making mistakes and won't be able to intervene as effectively. In an emotional state, our biofield weakens, and our resilience goes along with it. A telling event that our biofield is being challenged is when we become emotionally reactive and feel distress or tension in our body. The emotional realm has physically manifested top-down (mind to body) communication. Also, assertiveness and confidence slump, and we're no longer able to move ahead with precision, strength, and clarity. That doesn't feel good; plus we're not going to get the result we want.

When fear or doubt takes over, that lack of confidence can also put the brakes on our assertiveness. Second-guessing slows us down, and we might even freeze—a Polyvagal Theory concept, remember?—unable to take action and unable to make decisions and move forward. When a parent doesn't have much skill developed yet—or, even if they have skills, but they're running into brick walls and feeling discouraged—they're vulnerable to doubting themselves and making mistakes. If they get inconsistent responses from their child, the doubt and second-guessing can multiply. In my interpretation, all that questioning eventually blows out the biofield, weakening it and opening the door to more self-doubt.

As you can see in the following diagram, the three components of effective caregiving—skill, will, and biofield—do not exist in a vacuum; they are highly interdependent and interactive. A high level of *skill* increases our confidence, and confidence strengthens the *biofield*. The opposite is also true: a strong *biofield* vitalizes both one's *will* and one's *skills*. When a parent/caregiver gets to a certain level of energetic resilience—in other words, they've built up a strong biofield—they often find themselves more comfortable with their *skill* set. It gives them momentum too, and they might even feel a little excited—their desire and *will* are pumped—about what they're doing. They want to do the work. Sure, they might still be tired because it is hard work, after all, but they're doing it, and their biofield is a little stronger.

Whether we're new to the "job" of caregiving or we've been at it for a while, without the support of a healthy biofield, we'll inevitably get exhausted, our skills and abilities will be sub-par, and our willingness will hemorrhage as we try to be superheroes in the context of our already stressful and challenging world.

Which is to say that doing what we can to boost our energy field's resilience can help to lift everything else: grow our willingness and give us fuel to expand our skills. That's where energy psychology tools come in. EP is really fast, and you can do it at home. EP interventions

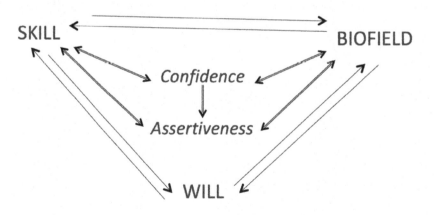

Higher skill levels, a strong will, and a healthy biofield each help support and build each other. With these resources at healthy levels, it becomes easier to lean on the logical, rational mind instead of emotional reactions when dealing with upsets and challenges

are designed specifically to neutralize charged thoughts which support a more resilient biofield, and once the biofield is strong, you are in a much better position to receive skills training and implement skills well, and that can give you confidence, which in turn helps amp up your willingness.

The Eight Caregiver Types

Now let's look at how these three areas of skill, will, and biofield intersect, interweave, and support each other and how they co-exist in a caregiver. Over the years, as I've worked with countless caregivers, I notice there's no way to predict where they are on the scale of being able to keep themselves centered, skilled, and effective at what they do. They could range from having a lot of skill, a lot of willingness, and strong biofield resilience to having low levels of all three—or be anywhere in between. I also noticed that people seem to fall into one of eight categories reflecting their levels of skill, will, and biofield strength. That's why I came up with the Caregiver Type Chart. It loosely defines eight caregiver types so anyone can identify the level of energy and the level of effectiveness they have, whether they're new to the role of caregiver or have been at it for years.

Once you identify which one of the eight types you currently are in the Caregiver Types Chart, you can get a better idea of where your weaknesses lie and what you can do to develop the three areas of skills. For example, maybe you've learned quite a few skills, and you do a good job of completing most of the tasks you set out to do, but you're just way too burned-out to nip problems in the bud or to be able to choose an optimal intervention when a situation arises. Or maybe you're passionate (a high degree of will) about the service you're providing, but your skills just aren't getting the job done successfully. The chart will help you to be honest about where you stand and what kind of results you can really expect from yourself in that state. With these insights, you empower yourself to reduce your stress, recharge, and be more effective at caring for others as well as yourself.

The chart for Caregiver Types lists the eight caregiver types. It plots out where you are with the three building blocks of caregiving—skill, will, and biofield resilience—and then tells you the good or not-so-good news about what results you can expect given where you are, how much of an impact you can make, and whether the good work you do is actually sustainable.

The caregiver types range from #1, which is not effective at all, to #8, which is both effective and sustainable.

In the Caregiver Types Chart, the second column reflects the typical frame of mind of a person at the level indicated in column one. The next three columns indicate where they are with their skills, will, and biofield strength. The sixth column reflects how that type does at responding to situations with their logical mind as opposed to falling back on reacting emotionally. The Sustainable? column reports on how sustainable that performance will be, given the levels of skills, will, and biofield strength for that caregiver type. After all, effectiveness is great, but if it's not sustainable, it's a lot less meaningful. The final column reveals the typical risks and the likely effectiveness and sustainability of someone operating at those levels.

Keep in mind that while most people will find themselves within one category or the other for a while, they can also change from day to day. You can have a good day at work, and you're feeling like a solid #8, but then problems might erupt, and you fall back into another level. It's normal for things to feel like they change.

Type 1. From Beginners to Burnt Out

This first caregiver type reflects the state of a person with low skills, low will, and a depleted biofield. They are not proficient in applied behavior analysis. They have little desire to do this type of work—or to even be in the industry, if they're a professional—and their biofield strength is low. As you might have guessed, they are not effective at doing what needs to be done, and their work won't be sustainable without some changes!

THE CAREGIVER TYPES

1	Either a beginner or burned out	LOW	LOW	LOW	HIGH	NO	*Exhausted* Not effective and not sustainable
2	I'm game	LOW	LOW	HIGH	HIGH	NO	Energetic reserves can only last for so long if skill and will are lacking
3	I can do this!	LOW	HIGH	HIGH	HIGH	NO	Lack of skill eventually wears away motivation and biofield resilience
4	Sweet grandmother	LOW	HIGH	LOW	HIGH	NO	Determination can only get you so far
5	Going through the motions	HIGH	LOW	LOW	HIGH	NO	Accomplishing things without personal involvement can exhaust reserves
6	I do this better than anyone— but I hate it	HIGH	LOW	HIGH	HIGH	NO	Lack of will and motivation will probably deplete biofield
7	Perfect on paper	HIGH	HIGH	LOW	HIGH	NO	With low biofield reserves, energy weakens. High performance is rarely sustained when pressure is perceived to be high
8	The Master	HIGH	HIGH	HIGH	LOW	YES	*Energized* Effective and sustainable

Keep in mind that if you're a #1, there's no reason to feel bad about it. How could parents of a first-born child with autism spectrum disorder possibly have great applied behavior analysis skills if they never had a need for them? After all, no one signed up for all of the extra parenting work that is demanded of them. It's also true that pretty much all professional caregivers, such as mental health professionals, teachers, and other school and community staff, start at this level, too. They just (hopefully) climb the chart a bit over the course of their career.

So this category isn't only about beginner parents. It can include parents, like many I've worked with, that have been doing a certain level of ABA for years and they're super burnt out. Their energy is running on fumes. And, being so depleted, they question their skills and their motivation. They might worry: "I still don't have enough training, and I am struggling emotionally to do this!" As we've seen, thoughts and emotions can influence the biofield, which supports healthy assertiveness, so that biofield is destined to fizzle out.

Some parents have learned some skills, but there are many that are still beyond their reach. For example, many of my private practice parents have lots of experience with ABA because they have children, now older, who were diagnosed with ASD at an early age. To troubleshoot a targeted behavior that they haven't had any success with using their current knowledge of ABA, I sometimes ask them to implement something new or different. This can sometimes increase their stress level and put them in fight/flight mode. They might fear that it's too hard for them to modify the practices they've gotten used to. Or, they might be afraid of the child's unpleasant consequences or the physical safety risks to their child or others when they introduce something new. Either way, the parent's willingness can plummet when they're asked to go beyond their comfort zone. Then, in true interdependent fashion, the low willingness will ding the skill performance, which can blow out the biofield, rendering the parent less effective than ever.

In sum, the low aptitude with skills snowballs and weakens one's will and one's energetic resilience. It's a very uncomfortable place to be in.

Type 2. I'm Game

This type describes a person with a low skill set, a low desire to want to do the work, yet they are blessed with high biofield strength. This person's attitude is typically, "Hey, I'm game. You know, I'll try this. I'm confident enough. I know I don't know what I'm doing, but heck, I'll do it." With just a smidge of willingness and low skill proficiency, the Type 2 caregiver will be at risk of making emotionally driven choices, which means they will work harder to get less satisfying results. It is likely that over time, their biofield will weaken and burn out.

Type 3. I'm Born To Do This! I Can Learn!

The third type is someone with a low skill set, a high desire to do this type of work, and a healthy, resilient biofield. This type, much like the last one, is still at risk of making emotionally driven choices, which will cut into their success, increase their doubts and thus weaken their biofield.

Some people who, deep down, feel that they were born to do this type of work often fit into this category. They want to say: "Train me! Mold me! I need to learn so I can do this effectively." People who are in an intense program of learning ABA can't avoid the fact that they are going to make a lot of mistakes in the beginning. There's a lot of room for error, and that can be psychologically stressful. They think, "I'm not learning fast enough. I'm not doing this well enough. I keep getting feedback that feels more critical than positive." Again, the person's confidence can get shaken, which snowballs into weakened assertiveness, and, ultimately, reduced resilience.

Type 4. Sweet Grandmother

This type reminds me of a sweet grandma that likes to say, "Oh, honey, I just want to make you feel good! Whatever it takes to make you happy, I'll do it!" She wants to help and love you, but she doesn't have a strong skill set to really deliver. In truth, these caregivers might want to make the person feel better, so *they* can feel better. This type of caregiver has a limited skill set and very little training; they have a lot of desire to do the work, but their biofield is running on fumes. Know anyone like that? Type 4 caregivers, too, are at risk of making emotionally driven choices, but not necessarily at the risk of weakening their biofield—because their biofield is weak to begin with!

Type 4 caregivers are fueled mostly by their emotions. That, again, increases their risk of making decisions emotionally instead of through an understanding of the scientific protocols and the structure of problem-solving within the ABA model. Some of them erroneously see ABA as being harsh. They don't understand that if you do ABA correctly, you're using reinforcement to change behavior, and that's not harsh at all. Warm and fuzzy hugs and loving gestures throughout the intervention won't make the therapy effective; in fact, they will impede its impact. And realistically, nobody in our culture can be a productive and healthy member of society without learning some limits.

Type 5. Going Through the Motions

The fifth caregiver type has acquired and developed a high level of ABA skills; it's the first time that we see that on the Caregiver Types Chart. Because of that foundation of skills and ability, they're less likely to fall back on emotional responses due to lack of skills than the previous four types, but there still remains some risk. Type 5 is a person who is highly trained and has good technique with ABA; they just don't *want* to do it. They aren't very motivated to do the work, and their biofield strength is low, too, so it won't be very resilient and, in fact, will continue to drain. The person is going through the motions, getting the job done, but not liking it, much less loving it. That can be incredibly exhausting. Exhaustion can contribute to making emotionally driven decisions, too.

Type 6. I Do This Better Than Anyone—But I Hate It

Type 6 caregivers have a high degree of skill, and they are highly trained with technical aspects of ABA. But, their willingness to do the work is low, even though their biofield strength is good. This is someone who likes to be "in the moment." Their attitude says, "Gosh darn it, I'm really good at this, and I know it. But I hate it, and I don't want to do it." They are at risk of weakening their biofield because they're prone to ruminating; they often go down the rabbit hole of thinking about other things they could be doing or want to be doing. But anyone with this make-up can't help but ask themselves at some point, "Why am I doing this? Do I have to do this? I just have to do it for X amount of time— and then I'll move on to something else." They've always got that end date in mind. They might be masterful enough that they don't respond to upsets emotionally very much, but their high level of skill and the strength of their biofield won't be able to sustain their work for the long term, either, leading to inner emotional turmoil.

Type 7. Perfect on Paper

Type 7 caregivers are highly adept at their work. They are motivated and have a strong desire to do the work, but they suffer from a sapped biofield. I always find this type of caregiver interesting. I know that an employer looking at their resumé would be impressed and want to hire them straight away, but what they can't see on paper is that with a depleted biofield, the person will have issues with confidence and assertiveness, and they're going to be very draining to have around. It is exactly where some of my staff were when I finally got a chance to sit down and talk with them. Their biofields started out nice and strong, but over time, their energy ran out, and that impacted every other type of performance.

Even Type 7s are at some risk of making decisions emotionally rather than logically when they begin to burn out. And most do burn out over time. They push themselves so hard that their energy eventually collapses, they have no reserves, and they get angry or just do whatever is easiest in the moment.

All eight of the caregiver types are served by taking direct steps to boost their biofield strength with energy psychology, but when it comes to Type 7s, it's the most important and perhaps the only thing to do. It's simply time to take care of *you*.

Type 8. The Master

Highly successful people in any industry and peak performers in any field are assuredly where they are due to the fact that they've optimized the three components of effectiveness: they've amassed high-level skills, they have both passion and will fueling what they're doing, and their biofields are healthy and strong. Likewise, caregiver Type 8s have an extensive toolbox of skills; they know what they're doing; they love doing what they do and who they do it with; and they are resilient, assertive, and confident.

Increasing Skill, Fortifying Will, and Strengthening the Biofield

Now it's time to find yourself on the chart! See how effective and sustainable you are currently, but, more importantly, find out where your gaps are so that you can begin building them up. How skilled are you? Assess your skill level. How motivated are you? Assess how engaged your will is. How's your energy? Find your biofield strength level on the grid above. Then make some decisions about what you want to target to keep yourself energized and effective at caring for your child.

Developing Skills

If you're lacking clinical skills that are specific to the ASD population, you can find a board-certified behavior analyst (BCBA), a licensed behavior specialist, or call your community support units wherever you live. They should have information for you about what trainings are offered, if there's any funding available, if it can go through your insurance, and anything else you need to know about adding to your ABA skills toolbox.

If you're already having trouble parenting your other children, too, a good place to start is outpatient therapy, which is available just about everywhere. Outpatient work can go a long way to help a parent get unstuck from emotionalizing situations, which helps them access their logical thinking mind more often when it comes to making a crucial decision. Outpatient therapists often know how to link you to community support programs, too.

Here are a few things I recommend you focus on as you add to your skill toolbox:

○ **Get specific**

When you begin to look more closely at your child's behaviors to figure out what's behind them, remember the four general functions of behaviors I described in chapter four. Remember that it's easy to fall into the trap of using cliché terms and fall back on assumptions when trying to understand what's motivating a child to behave poorly. If your kid is screaming at you and you're not experienced with applied behavior analysis, yet it's easy to characterize the child as being mad or "oppositional" or think that they're doing it because they want attention or they're not getting what they want. Remembering the four basic functions underlying actions and behaviors can help take the emotion out of your interpretations of behavior and can help you pin down the child's motivation much more accurately. The clearer you are about what functions are at play, the better your team can match the behavior with an effective and appropriate intervention.

Another tip about teasing out the function behind a behavior is to try to break down all the different behaviors that were expressed in an incident. A chain of events is not one thing; it's all those different events. So, if the kid's yelling at you, then he picks something up, then he throws something at you, and then he tries to run out the door—that's four behaviors, and all of them can have their own functions.

○ **Minimize prompt dependency**

Even if you don't have a lot of skill built up yet, you can reduce prompt dependency a lot by leaning on ABA's "three C's" to deliver that first directive as effectively as possible. Get their attention and communicate with simple, clear language. Regularly ask yourself, "Am I actually doing this for the kid instead of helping them learn to do it themselves? Am I helping too much? Am I helping every time they do what I'm asking?" If you do, then you need to take a step back and re-evaluate. If you've got professionals on your staff, it's a great question to discuss with them.

○ **Know that there's always more to learn**

Some parents that come to me have exhausted all other treatment facilities, centers, and behavioral specialists because they have mastered the behavior skills for their kids more than their providers have. But even they can benefit from some fine-tuning, which is what they come to me for. There are more tools out there that can help them. This is why it's so important to be honest with yourself about your skill level. I can't emphasize enough that, no matter how expert you think you are, it's still your kid, so it's hard to get around the emotional component that inevitably comes into play. You might want to consult with a professional to get a neutral opinion.

○ **Be super direct. Period.**

We all want to be compassionate with people who struggle in life. And, for the general population, communicating with compassion often means picking flowery words, using euphemisms, and talking all around a subject rather than talking directly to it. We might say, "You know, what I would really like is XYZ, so maybe we could work on that together sometime?" But that approach simply does not serve the ASD population well at all. They like simple, direct communication; they understand it better, and they are more comfortable with it. It's their comfort zone. To people in the ASD population, the "You know, what I would really like" approach is just way too much syntax. There are too many little words getting in the way of the important words. On the other hand, if they hear, for example, "There is a better way. This is the right way. Do this next time," it's a formula they can follow, a language they understand and know what to do with it. However, timing of the directness is also critical; choose a time when everyone is decompressed, and the child is ready to receive the information. To them, that is the compassionate way to communicate with them. They relax due to the directness, predictability, and rigidity of what is said. That's what makes them feel better. You're not being mean. For them, it's the ultimate kindness.

Developing Will

Willingness is something that no one else can give to you; if you aren't feeling it, you have to find it and nurture it within yourself. If your sense of willingness is low, there might be emotions at play. For example, if you're depressed because of how exhausted you are, you won't be as motivated as you used to be. Or you might be angry because you don't want to do what's in front of you. If that's the case, getting outpatient therapy for yourself might be of huge benefit to address emotions. Processing a lot of those feelings can be a first step and can help move the needle. Don't let yourself get away with thinking that you don't have the time and your needs don't come first. An hour of outpatient therapy once a week shouldn't be considered a luxury. It might be necessary. With the increasing convenience of telehealth, I urge you to consider it.

Developing your Biofield

The quickest, easiest, and probably most effective thing you can do to re-energize your biofield with respect to calming your thoughts and emotions is to use energy psychology tools like EFT, TFT, CEP, EMDR, MLT, HAT, and TAT. They're so doable, you can do them at home. They seem to help to deactivate your brain's amygdala—the safety-processing part of the brain—from its protective, reactive, fight/flight response, which otherwise makes us less effective at whatever we're trying to do. The #7 caregiver types, for example, are often very competitive and want everything to be perfect. Consumed with thoughts of: "It has to be better; It's never good enough," their amygdala is often overtaxed. All that intensity and stress causes their fuel levels to plummet. Energy psychology tools can help them get to the bottom of what drives them so hard so they can finally take their foot off the accelerator and rebalance. That's the way to be most effective, anyway.

If you don't want to go down the EP route, traditional therapy is another way to strengthen the biofield. Good therapy helps people decrease their somatic responses and helps them feel heard and validated and, as a result, confident. All those things help rebuild the energy field. I consider it the scenic route, however, because for this caregiver sub-population, time is of the essence.

When I did the study that I mentioned in the last chapter, once my staff realized what a difference being centered made for them in their work, it became amazingly effortless for them to maintain a strong biofield. Once they had worked for a while with the energy psychology tools I gave them, their work stopped being draining for them. They were able to build up a vocabulary of warning signals that their biofield strength was depleting, and that in turn built up their familiarity with and awareness of the nuances of what those warning signals felt like. As soon as they started to feel a little bit "off," they'd put in an "intervention" for themselves before the experience of feeling drained was able to build. So, caregivers really have to practice with these tools, ideally with someone giving them direction in the early stages. If they do, over time, their progress can improve their biofield enough to potentially influence someone else's. They get a benefit without feeling so drained.

Of course, keep in mind that it's still work. You don't get to be Superman or Superwoman. You have to keep working towards that balance.

As you learn EP methods, do remember that it's a journey. Be forgiving. In fact, the tools are forgiving in themselves; you don't have to do them perfectly to get results. And then there's often a roller coaster ride emotionally, as most people start out somewhat insecure with the process but soon discover what a difference they can make. That builds their confidence. Some people even get a little overconfident and have to deal with the inevitable crash when something doesn't go exactly right. As you fortify your biofield, some of this emotionalizing will fade, but it still is ideal if you have a mentor to practice with, to guide your learning path, and to give you context. Their help can be invaluable to get the methods to work for you as well as possible.

• • • • •

Now that you have an understanding of what will be the foundation of your well-being—your skill level, your will, and your energetic field—the next step is to up your game of self-care. That means finding ways to reduce your daily stress, taking steps to recharge your energy field, and plugging up the holes that allow your energy to drain. In the next chapter, I give you practical tips and powerful energy psychology tools you can do yourself so can feel energized once again.

8

Self-Care for Caregivers

How do we re-energize ourselves after we've gotten so depleted as caregivers? The good news is that when we learn tools and methods to finally dismantle some of the patterns and behaviors that are exhausting us and robbing us of clarity, certainty, and even joy, the energy we've been hungry for naturally begins to return and resurface. From my experience working with parents and caregivers, nine times out of ten, once they begin to dig themselves out of that energetic hole, they start to feel energized and alive again for the first time in a long time. It's as if they hadn't slept for days and then, after finally getting a full night's rest, they've woken up, maybe not fully recharged, but back in the driver's seat. There's been a qualitative shift. And that's when hope and confidence that they can manage their life and their ASD-diagnosed child's life finally begin to return.

But it is a process, and the first step is to do what is necessary to dig yourself out of the energetic hole you find yourself in. That means reducing your stress, bolstering your biofield, and learning methods that help prevent your energy from draining out so fast.

This whole book is designed to inform and empower you as a caregiver to bring you to the point of being able to re-energize and of getting your life back into your own hands again. The perspectives, guidelines, and exercises provided here are intended for you to take with you, use when you need, and, over time, help you reduce your stress significantly. But it's important to keep in mind that the tools and insights provided are not one-dimensional interventions to check off your checklist. It's not like going to therapy for six months and then thinking you're "done." Once you are strengthened and more centered by using them, you'll find it easier to set boundaries, set priorities, ask for what you need, and even do things you enjoy that energize you even more. You might not be able to schedule time to take yourself on a walk tomorrow, but as you gain the strength that this material gives you, you'll find you can in the future.

Put On Your Oxygen Mask

At the risk of sounding trite, I'm going to remind you of the proverbial flight attendant that tells us to put our oxygen mask on first before we attend to the needs of the children or any others that need help on the plane. Only then will you be fueled to help anyone else besides yourself. That's an important principle and bears repeating when it comes to self-care for caregivers. We absolutely need to put our own masks on first—and attend to our own need for destressing, incorporating healthy lifestyle habits, and even personal healing—before we're even close to being properly equipped to help anyone else.

Now, these days, we're inundated with messaging that tells us we should be taking better care of ourselves. "Eat more fresh foods." "Get a good night's sleep." "Get exercise." "Get out in nature." Even "pamper yourself" if you can. But most caregivers I work with tell me, "Sure, it would be nice to have some 'me time,' but the usual recommendations require time that I don't have!" The job of caregiving can be crazy overwhelming—as we've discussed in depth in earlier chapters. And those who attend to people with ASD can't simply add a few healthy-sounding tasks to a daily checklist with any confidence that they'll get done.

That's why this book is intended to help you see how critical it is that you attend to the "instrument" that does all of the caregiving—you. Getting recharged and re-energized requires that you do that. This chapter, in particular, provides simple techniques that won't take much time—I know you have little to spare—but can make a big difference. And if you remember that your own wellness can exponentially improve your decision-making, your mental clarity, your ability to be present to your child, and your ability to make the best choices in those worst-of-times moments, you'll understand that it's a small investment that pays you back over and over. Consider how much more you'd get done—and how much better you'd do it—if you felt energized and alive again.

Checklists Aren't For Everything

Now, let's talk about checklists. In the world of caregiving, checklists are a necessity, of course. Caregivers have so much chaos to manage that if they weren't a "checklist person" before they entered the alternate reality of caring for a young person with an autism spectrum disorder, they become one quickly. The only way for them to manage the chaos that has inserted itself into their lives is to take a more structured approach to most of the day's activities, and checklists help them do that.

But unfortunately, self-care just isn't one of those things you can put on a checklist. The things you do to take care of yourself can't just be accomplished by approaching them like they're one more checklist item—to be completed under pressure, usually mindlessly, and considered complete when the checkbox gets its checkmark. Sure, it might be practical for those just getting started as a caregiver to begin with a checklist approach to get the routine going. But eventually the more advanced energy exercises that I'll be sharing later in this chapter shouldn't be treated as just another checklist item. They're too foundational to your life for that. Self-care is a process, and it requires us to be present to ourselves so we can settle in, switch gears, and refuel and recharge on a lot of levels. I say this upfront to underscore the importance of thinking of self-care as switching gears because that's a huge part of it. When you can switch out of the fight/flight reactive modality and "flip the switch" over to being grounded, relaxed, and attending to your needs, that's when healing happens best.

Being locked into a checklist frame of mind can also do a disservice to caregivers because, once they look at their long list of to-do's, they tend to assume that they are the ones that will be performing all of them. Having a few skills under our belts and having learned some new information on the topic, it's easy to think that nobody can do the task better than we can, and we begin to minimize, ignore, or even forget that there's help and support available.

But given the exhausting nature of caregiving for those diagnosed with ASD, support is absolutely necessary.

Getting Support Wherever You Can

To help you survive the whirlwind of tasks to do, take the leap. Go through your to-do items and reconsider which ones you might be able to ask for help with. Think outside the box. Maybe another parent can help with carpooling of other kids in the family sometimes. Maybe you reach out to other local supports in the ASD community. We know that there might be safety issues when it comes to babysitting for our diagnosed child, so the trained parent or professional needs to be the one to do that. But maybe there are other things that people in the community can do to help you, such as deliver groceries or drive one of the other kids to soccer practice. How might some people help you with your household maintenance tasks? Begin to initiate conversations with your family and friends about how to approach what needs to be done in a way that is best for everybody concerned.

It's also helpful to remember that not everything has to be 100 percent perfect, so don't write people off because they can't do some things as well as you. Nobody's going to starve if the crayons aren't put away in order of color, right? In two-parent homes, I sometimes find that the parent leading the caregiving efforts doesn't recognize how much the "other" parent is actually willing to help. They might worry, justifiably, that if they hand over a task to their spouse, they won't be skilled enough to take care of certain details very well, so if the responsibility fell on their shoulders, they might cause damage or create more problems. And those problems would ultimately need to be cleaned up, which means you might end up being pulled into the job anyway. So, for those types of tasks, sure, it would not be wise to delegate them. But there are also many things that don't require perfection that others can handle sufficiently. And that means more time—maybe even more downtime—for the lead caregiver. A little flexibility goes a long way.

I also find that sometimes people feel ashamed that they can't do everything themselves; they feel they should be able to keep their house in order. Some conclude that, since they're home with their diagnosed child all day, they should be able to master their household duties at the same time. But—need I say it again?—being a caregiver of a child with ASD is simply a different ballgame. Don't minimize it, and don't judge yourself. You're in good company.

With so much on your plate, it's just time to get a little more assertive. If you're uncomfortable asking someone for help, try anyway. The worst they can do is say No. Now's the time to get more creative about how people can support you.

Setting Boundaries

While boundary issues can happen between any two people, they are especially problematic between a caregiver and the ASD-diagnosed child they're caring for. That means that imposing some boundaries early with that child is critical to your own good health. If you don't set boundaries with the child when they're young, the pattern will just be reinforced and maintained over the years, and your life will be forever without boundaries. The firehose of need will completely take over your life.

On the other hand, if you are applying a good set of applied behavior analysis skills and you have set limits from the beginning, it becomes less of an issue as the child gets older. For example, let's say Mom thinks it's cute when her four- or five-year-old remembers all the directions and the turns to drive to the health food store. It just happens to be a 45-minute drive. In fact, if Mom chooses the 30-minute route, the child throws a tantrum. After all, the 45-minute route is locked into the child's brain. It's the formula they've created for that trip, and they're comfortable with it. So, even though Mom could get there in 30 minutes, she takes the 45-minute drive to avoid an upset. But, think about it. If she takes the 45-minute route once a week for X number of years just to appease the child—well, you can do the math—that's a lot of time that gets forfeited in life. All because Mom avoided addressing the actual behavior and didn't set boundaries. Granted, this example can cause a safety issue in the car—all the more reason to seek early behavioral intervention.

I want to underscore the point that setting boundaries is not just a matter of being good for the parent; it's absolutely critical for the child's development. In the long run, the youngster will not be developing one of their primary executive functioning skills, namely, flexibility. That will have ramifications in many other areas of life. So, if the parent doesn't press on that flexibility early on, then their gap in that skill will be maintained and reinforced into and through adulthood.

Modifying Your Expectations for Your Child and Yourself

For most parents, as soon as they first learn of their child's diagnosis, they are struck with the weight of grief and loss. Dreams, hopes, and expectations for their child's life are dashed, and they begin to see their wishes for their child to be successful in life as misguided fantasies that will never see the light of day. They are in a whirlwind of worry: *Will my kid be able to have a family? Will they be able to join the workforce? Will they be able to make friends and feel accepted in public life?* They don't know the answer to these questions; the expectations they've heralded for their child will have to change.

If you have a child that is demonstrably different from the norm in some way, you inevitably have to wrestle with the dilemma of what expectations you're going to have for the way they engage with the world. Should you focus on having them adapt to the expectations of the community and learn new skills to do that? Or should the community be the one to "give a little" and make adjustments for your child? Should the square peg soften its edges to fit in the round hole, or should the round hole learn to embrace the square peg? You have to decide if you want your child to fit in and function as best as they can in the world as it is—with all the judgments, misperceptions, and harshness that come with it—or if you want to support your child being 100 percent who they are, and you want the world to fit itself around them. Or maybe there's a choice somewhere in the middle. After all, we can't control whether or not others change, but we can work with the child to adapt.

Nowadays, we are seeing more public outcry for acceptance of all sorts of personal expression that have been cultural outliers in our society for a long time. People from diverse racial backgrounds, gender identities, sexual preferences, and so on are seeking recognition and inclusion more than ever. It's encouraging, sure. But when it comes down to real-life interactions with our ASD-diagnosed child, we caregivers have to remember that the world just isn't very kind all the time. And, as much as people are advocating for more acceptance, many others resent it. So, we want to be realistic. If you want your child to fit into society as it is and as comfortably as possible, then learning and mastering ABA and the other skills I mentioned earlier will be your best tools to set them up for success.

Still, the question is: What new expectations *should* we hold for our ASD-diagnosed child? The truth is, we never really know *how* our child's future will be different from our expectations. Just because they have been diagnosed with ASD doesn't mean they can't do this, and they'll never have that. In fact, there might be many new opportunities available to them by the time they grow up, things that you didn't think were possible because they don't exist today. Plus, some kids who are profoundly affected with ASD can still accomplish tremendous achievements if they've gone through a high-quality ABA program and have developed a useful and adaptable skillset. Several clients of mine could barely speak some years ago, but now they're college bound, or they're on their way to graduate from college with degrees, and they will be well equipped to enter the workforce relatively successfully.

Ultimately, we want to be realistic about the grief we feel as well as the loss of our early innocent hopes and expectations for our child. But we can also remember that technology is changing a lot of things and making a lot of things possible for people. I also like to remind parents I work with to think about their *own* parents' expectations for them. Did they fulfill them lock, stock, and barrel? Or did they do their own thing? It's actually quite common for parents to have to adapt to what the child can do and wants to do with their lives. It's often healthy to support the child in living the life that suits them rather than making choices their parents prefer. Many parents I work with want their children to get married, largely because they want to make sure they weren't alone in life and that they'd have support. But some young adults really don't want to get married when they realize the flexibility required and compromises involved. I ask these parents, "Wait. Whose needs are we discussing? Your kid is independent and happy. Let them make their own choices."

The Most Helpful Attitude? Imperfection Happens.

As you begin to build your skillset and discover what amazing results your tools can get for you, you start to build confidence and hope. In fact, in the short term, it's easy to get a little overconfident as you see things finally working for you. But then you inevitably hit a brick wall. Nothing lasts forever, right? You'll run into seemingly insurmountable obstacles again. Either you can't fit a tool that you have into the problem, or a tool you have doesn't fix the problem. Then, in that moment or over a short period of time, you might start mentally racking up your "failures" and start to doubt all of your abilities. The doubts mount, and you are soon falling headfirst into a downward spiral of uncertainty, indecision, negativity, and over-questioning.

The key to softening these blows and preventing yourself from getting too far down that rabbit hole is to know that you're going to make mistakes. Misinterpretation is going to happen; there are going to be communication errors. I hear so many caregivers talking "woulda, shoulda, coulda." They beat themselves up for this or that—something that they didn't do as well as they wanted to. Maybe they didn't catch the antecedent soon enough. But I have to remind them they're only human.

You might have gotten very comfortable with a certain set of skills working for you, but the day they don't work, don't beat yourself up about it. You need to fix it, move past it, and try not to let the emotions get the upper hand. You can't take them too seriously. Stay in logical mind as much as possible.

The Place for Mindfulness and Meditation

There are countless books on mindfulness in the marketplace, and it's not my primary goal for you to gain mastery of this concept here. Very briefly, I consider it a valuable practice in general and a high priority for caregivers to be mindful and present to their experience as much as possible. When I introduced energy psychology to my staff at Highlands Hospital Regional Center for Autism, they reported the difference that mindfulness made in doing their jobs well. That was their "flipping-the-switch" superpower that I described in chapter six. First, when things got somewhat squirrelly, they'd notice that their brains were headed in a less-than-helpful direction. That "noticing" was mindfulness. Then they say to themselves something like, "But I'm not going there. I need to come back to what I'm doing right now," or remind themselves to pay attention to what was happening. This helped them get back to being present, out of their emotions if any were coming up, and back accessing their logical mind, so they functioned better and made better decisions.

Many have found that when those doubts start to rear their heads, and you begin to spiral down the rabbit hole, mindfulness can help you wake up and notice that it's happening. Then, if you can begin to recognize the doubt as it happens, you can begin to intentionally insert some of the energy psychology tools I teach later in this chapter. As I've described previously, if and when things break down, your emotional brain can kick you into that fight/flight state—which is energetically draining. But mindfulness helps you stop that emotional brain train before it completely derails you.

What about meditation? I consider meditation to be a super-advanced skill. It's actually very hard to do for a lot of people, but, unfortunately, there's a social media stigma at the same time that says that everyone should be doing it. Then, that gets interpreted as "everyone can do it." But that's not true. Not everyone can.

In general, I don't recommend a focus on meditation to my families because of how difficult it is to do and because it can be very time-consuming to learn and practice it. Plus, if mindfulness is like several short walks during the day, meditation is a distance run when it comes to taking steps to quiet the mind. Popular approaches start with blocking out mind "noise" to focus on one specific thing, which might be easy for 20 seconds, but 20 minutes can be extremely difficult. Most people thought jump or fall asleep. Mindfulness, on the other hand, has to do with practicing short snippets of bringing awareness to the moment and paying attention to your actions in the present. Additionally, mindfulness is bringing awareness to our internal dialogue, or "self-talk." Self-talk can be negative or positive; bringing attention to whatever the dialogue says and reframing it to encourage rational statements can go a long way. It's one of the skills you learn in ABA, and it can be incredibly valuable when you need to make choices.

Thoughts About Custody Arrangements

While it's not directly a self-care topic, I want to write briefly about custody arrangements because it can be a cause of tremendous stress for parents. Custody arrangements can be difficult for just about any child, but for the ASD population, it can be especially harsh. After all, change can be challenging for almost all of us, but for the ASD population, it's even more so. Those with ASD almost always have a tremendous reliance on formulas and on having repeated experiences they can rely on, so being forced to go back and forth between households can overwhelm them with sensory overload that they won't be able to process well. In many instances, the visits are not going to be all that happy. It can also take this population a little bit longer to readjust once they are back where they started. This means if the child is with Mom for a few days and then Dad for a few days, by the time they get back to Mom's and take two days to adjust, it's time for them to pick up and go back to Dad's. Generally, these kids function best with a high level of structure and familiarity; they want to know what's next, so being forced to uproot every few days or weeks can be extremely disruptive and disturbing to them.

If you're a parent sharing custody, I recommend that you be honest with yourself about how your child is managing the situation and whether it's hurting them more than necessary. More than anything, I strongly advise people to try and do what's best for the child, even if that means not getting some of their own preferences fulfilled. Further, if it's possible to get uninfluenced and authentic input from the child, do that, and factor it in as you weigh the options available to you.

Self-Care Exercises for Caregivers

In the early days of my career, Dr. Nicosia trained me to do some foundational exercises. One in particular, originally created by the originator of Thought Field Therapy, psychologist Roger Callahan, helped get the body and mind in a more optimal state to receive subsequent intervention treatments. As I worked with people with trauma, head injuries, and all sorts of neurological problems, I saw that it helped center and prep the body and brain, essentially, so they're better able to recondition the body/mind and establish a more functional way of operating in the world. And although there may not be any formal studies on using what I would consider readiness tools alone, I find that these techniques improve outcomes of any subsequent energy work that engages with the meridians especially.

Take inventory for a moment. Do you feel like you've experienced extremely high stress levels that drained you to the bone? Would it be fair to say that you—yes, you—have experienced trauma, whether from hearing the diagnosis, from some interaction with your child, or witnessing some of your child's behavior in the community? If you're a parent or caregiver of a child with ASD, it's highly likely that you have experienced trauma. Otherwise, why would you be reading this book?

"Trauma" refers to the distress as a result of ongoing events that are physically or emotionally harmful with lasting adverse effects on the person's ability to function mentally, socially, emotionally, and/or spiritually whereas a traumatic event is an occurrence that led to distress. More specific definitions and criteria are found in the DSM-V. Trauma causes complex effects in the human energy system, which is why it's so important to be aware of it. Joe's trauma response for a specific event is not the same as Janette's trauma response for the same specific event. Trauma is highly individualized and subjective.

The self-care methods I provide below are intended to help you begin to get out from under the grip of the fight/flight/freeze mode that you've come to know as your new normal. But the human psyche is extraordinarily challenging and complex, so no energy psychology method is going to be a silver bullet and fix everything with one swallow. These methods can hold tremendous value, so learn them, try them, use them, and get as much benefit as you can from them.

If you have been traumatized by your situation, then also consider finding a well-trained, licensed mental health practitioner who treats trauma to help you go deeper and release some of what is holding your trauma in place. They might use some of the energy techniques I've mentioned before, such as EFT, TFT, EMDR,, HAT, and TAT, for example, and be instrumental in helping you to lighten the burden of your trauma and to free up a lot of the energy that's locked within. However, I do encourage you to work with a licensed professional with clinical experience treating trauma. These professionals have the full scope of trauma-treatment based tools that are required to comply with ethical standards that ensure your emotional safety.[13]

The exercises I offer here are foundational exercises and pretty safe for most people. Realistically, we're not asking them to do miracles for us or heal long-standing emotional pain or trauma. These are simple sequences for securing a foundation for your inner health. They won't take a deep dive into your internal energy pathways—what Traditional Chinese Medicine and energy psychology practitioners call "meridians." It's better to do that with a professional with clinical expertise

---

13 I recommend that anyone practicing energy psychology get familiar with this valuable book: Feinstein, D., & Eden, D. (2011). *Ethics handbook for energy healing practitioners: A guide for the professional practice of energy medicine and energy psychology.* Elite Books.

and who is well informed about your specific issue. But they can help you shift your energy in your body, so you feel the difference.

I recommend that you do these exercises in the order I present them here; it is the most conservative approach. First, master the Collarbone Breathing technique and then the Over-Energy Correction. Then, do the Safety Reversal and/or the Possibility Reversal. It's best if you incorporate these breathing exercises into your daily routine, perhaps even doing them more than once daily. Consistency is key. Over time, you might find that they become welcome friends that you rely on every day.

It's also helpful to rate how you feel before and after you do an exercise so you can get a quantitative idea of any improvements you experienced. For that, I recommend the Subjective Units of Disturbance Scale, or SUDS, a scale that ranges from 0 to 10 to measure the degree of distress you are experiencing. In other words, you'd rate something a 0 if you're feeling no disturbance or upset and feel completely free of anything stressful in your body. You'd rate it a 10 if you're in the worst pain, distress, or anxiety you've ever had in your life.

Checking in with yourself and rating your SUDS is also helpful as a mindfulness exercise on its own. Any time you want, you can go inside and do a body scan: See what you notice from the top of your head down through your torso and through your feet. Do you have stress or pain or tension anywhere? If so, what number would you give it on a scale of 0 to 10?

Then, before doing one of the exercises below, take your SUDS, and then take it again afterward. Did your stress, pain, or tension reduce compared to the first set of numbers? Is it higher? Did it stay the same? The numbers can give you a bit more of a quantitative sense of how well the method worked for you. Over just a little bit of time, you'll likely find that you can do quite a lot to lower your feelings of being stressed and overwhelmed.

SUDS provides interesting feedback in its own right, too. After I work with someone for a month or so, it's almost predictable that they will tell me they realize that they have been minimizing their stress levels. Now that they have a rating instrument and tools to reduce their anxiety, they realize that their SUDS numbers in the past were probably a lot higher than they had been willing or able enough to acknowledge or fully identify. And now, because they've been doing the techniques, they're experiencing lower levels, too.

Collarbone Breathing Technique

Upon recent consultation, Joanne M Callahan, MBA, President, Callahan Techniques, Ltd. explained this technique.

> The collarbone breathing exercise was developed as a neurological alignment procedure to accomplish the corrections achieved by cranial sacral manipulation and the switching referred to in Applied kinesiology. Dr. Callahan developed this procedure while working with George Goodheart on severely disturbed mental patients with George using cranial sacral manipulation and Roger developing something that could be safely self-applied and accomplish the same corrections.
>
> The collarbone breathing is a very effective balancing procedure. It works like the cogs in the wheel of a bicycle. If the cogs are aligned, the bicycle moves forward with ease and leverage. If you hit a rock or curb and the cogs become misaligned, the bicycle will still move forward but it will be a difficult jerky movement. This is what happens to us in daily life. It is especially useful for all types of anxiety, and when aligned, everything else works better.

Follow the instructions below, or you can watch me walk you through it on YouTube at https://www.youtube.com/watch?v=hIu5t-TdiRrA.

1. Find the little round notch at the innermost edge of one of your collarbones with one of your hands. Move that hand down about one inch, and then lay it flat against that side of your chest.

2. As you hold that hand there, you're going to tap the back of that hand with the other hand. The spot to tap is about half-

way down from the knuckles toward the wrist and along an imaginary line between the pinky and ring finger. Tap fairly quickly and lightly.

3. While tapping, take a deep breath in and then let it out.

4. Take another deep breath in and hold it in for 5-10 taps.

5. Let half of the breath out and hold that for 5-10 taps.

6. Breathe out the rest of the air from your lungs for 5-10 taps.

7. Take half a breath in and hold it for 5-10 taps.

8. Release the breath.

9. Move the hand that you placed in Step 1 to the other side, about an inch down from that collarbone notch.

10. Repeat Steps 2 through 8 above.

11. Now, take your other hand and place it on either of the spots beneath the collarbone described above. It doesn't matter which side you choose because, like the first half of the exercise, you'll do the same thing on both sides. Repeat steps 2 through 10, only this time, the hands are taking opposite roles.

12. Now, do the whole routine over again—steps 2 through 10—only this time with the "holding" hand in a fist position, that is, the thumb inside the four fingers. When you place your fist against your body, the back of your hand should face outward. Repeat with the opposite fist.

The Over-Energy Correction Technique

Some of my clients like to call this technique the "Pretzel." It is historically known as "Cook's Hookup" since it is a modified version of a method developed by Wayne Cook and is also referenced in *Brain Gym* by Paul and Gail Dennison. Dr. Nicosia originally taught me to modify the original to best suit a person's handedness from his early diagnostic trainings. The following instructions are written for those who are right-handed. If you are left-handed, then use the opposite sides in steps 1 and 3.

1. Cross your left foot or ankle over your right.

2. Place your arms out in front of you, hands back to back.

3. Cross your right hand over your left.

4. Clasp your fingers together.

5. Bring your hands toward your chest, elbows low, loosening fingers and shoulders, so they're comfortable.

Breath for two minutes, inhaling through your nose and exhaling through your mouth. If it is difficult for you to breathe that way, place your tongue against the roof of your mouth when you inhale and drop the tongue when you exhale. The tongue positions will help force the breath in through your nose and out through your mouth.

The Safety and Possibility Reversals

Like the Collarbone Breathing technique, the concept of the psychological reversal was originated by Roger Callahan. Suzanne Connolly, LCSW, LMFT, LISAC is a long time TFT practitioner who trains mental health therapists and others to help worldwide victims of national disasters and who has authored and co-authored three studies using TFT with victims of genocide. According to Suzanne, "Callahan's main reversal, his first discovery, was tapping small intestine 3 (SI-3) on the side of the hand. He called it "the mini" when it had to be used at a certain time during treatment." There are many types of reversals and identifying and treating them can be complex. Fred Gallo, Ph.D., a leader in the energy psychology field, recently described to me the history of reversal types. He originally found the first variation of a reversal involving "deserving." Then Sandi Radomski, N.D. stumbled upon the idea of "safety" in one of his workshops. Later, Gallo found more variations in Callahan's original concepts of reversals, which Gallo called "Criteria Related Reversals."

Gallo then collaborated with James Durlacher on what Durlacher called "Degrees of Reversals" and they found that each of their growing lists of reversal types had similarities. I find two of them particularly effective for caregivers—the Safety Reversal and the Possibility Reversal. These can be practically understood as what happens when someone holds a belief that something isn't "safe" or that something isn't "possible" even if that might not be true. If you are a TFT practitioner, you will see how Callahan's Deep Level and Specific Reversal concepts are relevant.

Many people, especially those caring for a child with ASD, harbor fears of not being safe and/or fears that sustained, positive change is not a real possibility. Other times, to protect us and keep us safe, our brains trick us into extreme thinking. I see this so often in caregivers of kids with ASD. At some point, they have told themselves—either consciously or subconsciously, in other words, the belief has been embedded without their knowing—that their kid will not be safe unless something very specific happens or doesn't happen. They've amassed a whole collection of "have-to's" that begin to rule their lives. Examples are: " I have to walk my kid across the street every time," "I have to drive the long, 45-minute route to the health food store," "I can't let that other person help me because if they don't do it exactly like I do it, I don't know my child will be safe," or "I have to triple-lock the doors so my child can't get out of the house by themselves."

Adding to the pressure is the fact that ABA repeatedly emphasizes the need for safety—which is appropriate—but the effect is that it can reinforce those fears.

That constant emphasis on vigilance about safety, along with all of the disaster-preventing "rules" that one's collected, can end up getting the best of you. Hoping to use those rules to keep everyone safe and to keep disaster at bay, the pattern ends up doing you a lot of harm if sustained over long periods of time. So, putting these safety "controls" aside at the right time is a great first step in helping your body and mind dispel the beliefs. Once out of that state, you will think more clearly, see more options, respond more effectively, and rely on the skills that you've taken the time and effort to develop. These corrections are also helpful as a foundation for any other energy psychology methods you use, making them more impactful, more quickly.

The Safety Reversal

The Safety Reversal technique helps the body recognize that, just because we want to be aware, it doesn't mean that our life or somebody else's life is in danger every single moment. It helps us tell our body and brain that we're OK with the fact that parts of ourselves have tried to preserve safety at all costs, but we just don't really need to work that hard in order to do so. We can relax.

1. Place your two hands in front of you, palms up, with the outside of the hands against each other.

2. Tap the outside edges of your hands lightly together. As you tap, continue to Step 3:

3. Say the following out loud three times: "I accept myself and all of my parts even if some of my parts might not feel like it's safe to be over this problem."

The Possibility Reversal

As I've described in detail, the life of a caregiver of a child with ASD can be quite overwhelming and feel burdensome, and it's easy for people to start thinking, "This will never end. I'll never be able to get over all this stress. This is now my lifestyle, and it has to be, and that's not going to change." The Possibility Reversal can be used to lighten these types of feelings.

1. Place your two hands in front of you, palms up, with the outside of the hands against each other.

2. Tap the outside edges of your hands lightly together. As you tap, continue to Step 3:

3. Say the following out loud three times: "I accept myself and all of my parts even if some of my parts might not feel like it's possible to be over this problem."

Feel free to combine the Safety and Possibility Reversals. If you're working with a trained professional, you can name the problem more specifically. For example, if someone felt like they just can't let go of any responsibilities in order to lighten their workload, they might word their reversal like this:

"I accept myself and all of my parts even if some of my parts might not feel like it's safe or possible to be over this problem of being able to relinquish some of my responsibilities."

◆ ◆ ◆ ◆ ◆

As a caregiver, you cannot forget that you are the instrument of care and that your health, balance, resilience, and sanity are just as important as your knowledge and skills when it comes to taking care of the endless number of things that need to be done. I hope that the information in this book has given you helpful insights into some of the most effective treatment techniques in the industry, a greater appreciation for the huge task you've taken on as a caregiver, and a deeper resolve to take care of yourself in the process. I also hope that you've learned that you do have the power to reclaim your energy—and your life!

Acknowledgments

There was definitely a specific chain of people in my professional career that made this book possible. Dr. Greg Nicosia led me to Carole Stern, Dr. David Gruder, and Dr. Fred Gallo. Carole led me to Cleveland Clinic and Travis Haycook. Dr. David led me to Randy Peyser who embraced the idea for my book and then to my editor Diane Eaton who was invaluable in shaping my message! Special thanks also to Joanne Callahan, Suzanne Connolly, and Dr. Caleb Bupp.

I owe appreciation to my Grandmother, Mary, who from the time I was a little girl said, "You should write a book someday"—though I never saw it coming.

And this book is dedicated to my parents who, during my entire life, have encouraged me to stand against the status quo.

Index

A

"A Cartography of Energy Medicine: From Subtle Anatomy to Energy Physiology" (Leskowitz), 111
Active training, experiencing, 11
Activity reinforcers, 55–56
Addict phase, 66–67
Adelphoi Village, at-risk children (assessment/treatment/supervision), 14
Advanced Diagnostics, P.C., 4, 5
Advanced Integrative Therapy (AIT), 108
Affective regulation, 31
Antecedent-Behavior-Consequence (ABC), usage/model, 49–50, 116
Antecedent, determination, 48
Anterior cingulate cortex, social-emotional/ cognitive functions (association), 31
Anxiety, 88
  diagnosis, 15–16, 63
  increase, 96
  treatment, 9
Applied Behavior Analysis (ABA), 21, 46
  adjustment, 93–95
  Antecedent-Behavior-Consequence (ABC), usage, 49–50
  application, 47–48
  building-block approach, 61–63
  clear, concise, and consistent (three Cs), 49, 116, 131–132
  concerns, 63–66
  design, 62
  experience, 126
  methodology, 63–64, 76
  methods, usage, 24, 65
  modality, 47
  skills, 126, 128
  skills toolbox, 130
  technical aspects, training, 128–129
  treatment, 48–50
  understanding, 23–24
  usage, 48, 66–68, 115
Asperger's disorder, diagnosis, 9, 10, 29, 30
Assertiveness, emotional charge, 120–121
Assessment
  future, 32–37

tools, 69
Association for Comprehensive Energy Psychology (ACEP), EP definition, 109–110
Attention
  executive functioning skill, 38, 40–41
  issues, 72
Attention Deficit Hyperactive Disorder (ADHD), 9, 15–16
Attention, improvements, 11–12
Attention-seeking function, 74, 76
Autism, 27
  APA definition, ix
  diagnosis, 9, 28, 42–43
  DSM-IV characterization, 28
  DSM meaning, 27–28
  genetic diagnosis answer, finding, 36
  treatment, 13
Autism Diagnostic Interview-Revised (ADI-R), 22
Autism Diagnostic Observation Schedule (ADOS) assessment, 22
Autism spectrum
  child rules, 89
  treatment, 37–38
Autism spectrum disorder (ASD), 27
  ASD-related challenges, 23
  attention, 138
  brain symmetry, examination, 33
  characterization, 31
  children, real-life interactions, 143
  complexity, x, 14–15
  confusion/misinformation, 27
  definition, fluidity, 30
  diagnosis, vii, 62, 88, 126
    emotional impact, 95–97
    numbers, increase, x
    shock/disappointment, facing (difficulty), 95
  diagnostic category, creation, 29
  formulas, value, 45
  heterogeneous nature, 33
  impact, viii
  incidence, increase, viii
  overstimulation response, 65–66
  population, performance, ix

About the Author

MANDI FREGER, M.ED., DCEP, LBS, LPC is a seasoned clinical practitioner with over 25 years of experience in both the treatment of Autism Spectrum Disorder and the practice of Energy Psychology techniques. Freger was featured as an expert panelist in the documentary "The Science of Tapping," a first of its kind to discuss the science behind the technique of meridian based therapies or treating mental health ailments.

Freger's long-time mentors include Dr. Greg Nicosia, Dr. Fred Gallo, and Carole Stern who were among Dr. Roger Callahan's first students in the early 1990s. Dr. Callahan was responsible for founding the implementation of the acupuncture meridians to treat emotional problems. Another of Dr. Callahan's students, Gary Craig, broke away and created a more simplified version of what most people now know to be Emotional Freedom Techniques or EFT.

She has been a long-time speaker at The Association for Comprehensive Energy Psychology (ACEP). As their Education Director, she assisted with gaining approval to offer CE credits for ACEP's courses, specifically from the American Psychological Association (APA). ACEP was the premier organization to obtain this standing by the APA for these types of modalities. It was then followed by the scientific methods and practices in the field of Energy Psychology to rapidly heal extreme emotional stress and trauma.

With her extensive experience in the treatment of Autism Spectrum Disorder, Freger was in the unique position to be hired as the Director of Autism Services of the first affiliate program through Cleveland Clinic Children's Hospital to build a center-based program and diagnostic facility for ASD from the inception.

In 2019 she hosted her own radio show on Bold Brave Media Global network called *The Energy of Autism*, that reached iHeart radio and iTunes audiences. An episode of a media presentation was with Paula Shaw on San Diego's *Change It Up Radio*, which has a reach of over 200,000 listeners.

Mandi Freger is licensed as a professional counselor and a behavioral specialist in PA. She holds a master's degree in educational psychology and a diplomat in comprehensive energy psychology. She also has basic training in Integrative and Functional Medicine through the Institute for Functional Medicine. Additionally, she is a group fitness instructor for cycling, Zumba®, and yoga.

More information can be found at www.mandifreger.com